studysync®

Reading & Writing Companion
British Literature

UNIT 6

studysync.com

Send all inquiries to:
BookheadEd Learning, LLC
610 Daniel Young Drive
Sonoma, CA 95476

ISBN 978-1-97-016226-4

2 3 4 5 6 LMN 24 23 22 21 20

B

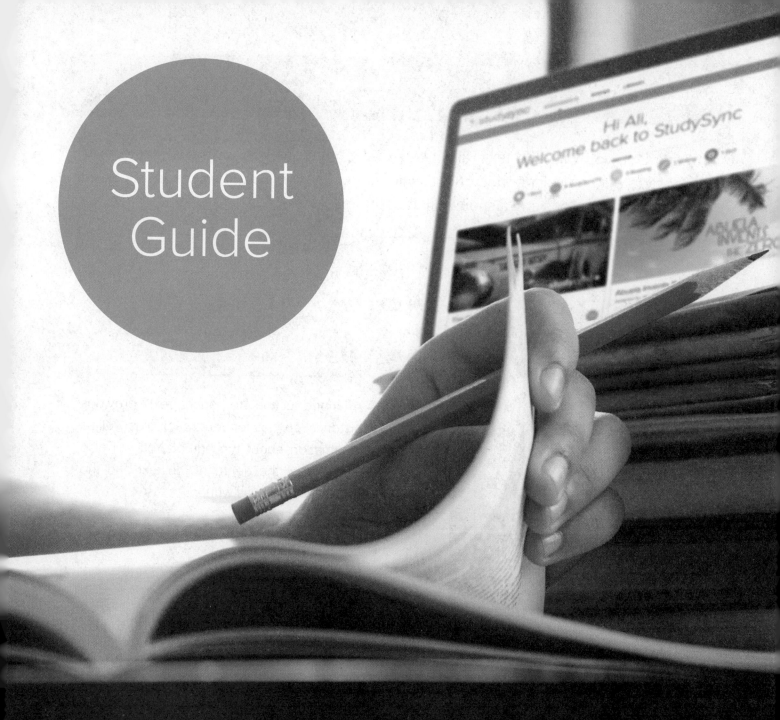

Student Guide

Getting Started

Welcome to the StudySync Reading & Writing Companion! In this book, you will find a collection of readings based on the literary focus of the unit you are studying. As you work through the readings, you will be asked to answer questions and perform a variety of tasks designed to help you closely analyze and understand each text selection. Read on for an explanation of each section of this book.

Close Reading and Writing Routine

In each unit, you will read texts and text excerpts that are from or are in some way connected to a particular period of British literature. Each reading encourages a closer look through questions and a short writing assignment.

1 Introduction

An Introduction to each text provides historical context for your reading as well as information about the author. You will also learn about the genre of the text and the year in which it was written.

2 Notes

Many times, while working through the activities after each text, you will be asked to **annotate** or **make annotations** about what you are reading. This means that you should highlight or underline words in the text and use the "Notes" column to make comments or jot down any questions you have. You may also want to note any unfamiliar vocabulary words here.

You will also see sample student annotations to go along with the Skill lesson for that text.

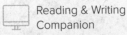

3 First Read

During your first reading of each selection, you should just try to get a general idea of the content and message of the reading. Don't worry if there are parts you don't understand or words that are unfamiliar to you. You'll have an opportunity later to dive deeper into the text.

4 Think Questions

These questions will ask you to start thinking critically about the text, asking specific questions about its purpose, and making connections to your prior knowledge and reading experiences. To answer these questions, you should go back to the text and draw upon specific evidence to support your responses. You will also begin to explore some of the more challenging vocabulary words in the selection.

5 Skills

Each Skill includes two parts: Checklist and Your Turn. In the Checklist, you will learn the process for analyzing the text. The model student annotations in the text provide examples of how you might make your own notes following the instructions in the Checklist. In the Your Turn, you will use those same instructions to practice the skill.

---

3 First Read

Read "The Pardoner's Prologue." After you read, complete the Think Questions below.

☁ THINK QUESTIONS

1. In stanza two, the Pardoner says, "Our liege-lord's seal on my patent perfect, / I show that first, my safety to protect, / And then no man's so old, no priest nor clerk, / As to disturb me in Christ's holy work." What can you infer about the Pardoner's attitude about the bulls, or official public decrees, that he carries? What purpose do they serve for him? Cite evidence from the text to support your explanation.

2. What are the two relics, or religious objects imbued with miraculous powers, that the Pardoner discusses? What are the specific alleged powers of these seemingly banal objects, according to the Pardoner? Cite evidence from the text to support your answer.

3. Citing the Pardoner's own words, what do you think he is most concerned about? How deeply is he invested in the salvation of his congregants?

4. The Latin word *pater* means "father." With this information in mind and using context clues from the text, write your best definition of the word **patriarch** here.

5. What is the meaning of the word **avarice** as it is used in the text? Write your best definition here, along with a brief explanation of how you arrived at its meaning.

The Pardoner's Prologue (from *The Canterbury Tales*)

5 Skill: Point of View

Use the Checklist to analyze Point of View in "The Pardoner's Prologue." Refer to the sample student annotations about Point of View in the text.

••• CHECKLIST FOR POINT OF VIEW

To grasp a character's point of view in which what is directly stated is different from what is really meant, note the following:

✓ Literary techniques intended to provide humor or criticism. Examples of these include:

- Sarcasm, or the use of language that says one thing but means the opposite.
- Irony, or a contrast between what one expects to happen and what happens.
- Understatement, or an instance where a character deliberately makes a situation seem less important or serious than it is.
- Satire, or the use of humor, irony, exaggeration, or ridicule to expose and criticize people's foolishness or vices.

✓ Possible critiques an author might be making about contemporary society through theme or characters' actions and words.

✓ An unreliable narrator or character whose point of view cannot be trusted.

To analyze a case in which grasping a point of view requires distinguishing what is directly stated in a text from what is really meant, consider the following questions:

✓ When do you notice that the reader's point of view differs from that of the character or speaker in this text?

✓ How does a character's or narrator's point of view contribute to a nonliteral understanding of

---

⟳ YOUR TURN

1. The Pardoner uses figurative language when he states "To spice therewith a bit my sermoning / And stir men to devotion, marvelling. . ." Why does the Pardoner use this metaphor?

○ A. He uses the metaphor to explain how he makes his sermons more appetizing so he can better trick the churchgoers.
○ B. He uses the metaphor to explain the process of using potions and relics in the forgiveness of sin.
○ C. The metaphor serves to educate the churchgoers.
○ D. He uses the metaphor to persuade the churchgoers.

2. Which of the following phrases make it clear that the Pardoner knows he is a liar?

○ A. "And, good sirs, it's a cure for jealousy;"
○ B. "Shall every sheep be healed that of this well / Drinks but one draught"
○ C. "Then show I forth my hollow crystal-stones,"
○ D. "Relics are these, as these, they think, every one"

3. This question has two parts. First, answer Part A. Then, answer Part B.

Part A: Which statement best reflects the relationship the Pardoner has with the churchgoers?

○ A. He respects them and seeks their advice on religious matters.
○ B. He tries to manipulate them and hide his true intentions.
○ C. He tries to help them but is concerned they won't accept it.
○ D. He believes they are intelligent but immoral.

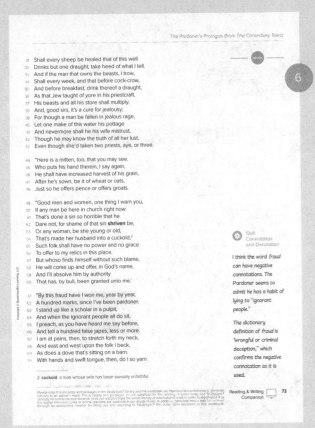

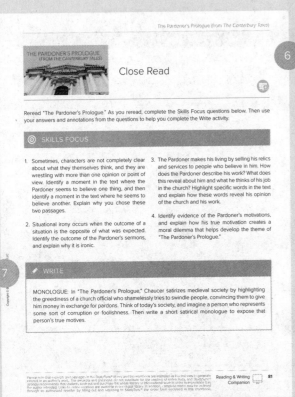

6 Close Read & Skills Focus

After you have completed the First Read, you will be asked to go back and read the text more closely and critically. Before you begin your Close Read, you should read through the Skills Focus to get an idea of the concepts you will want to focus on during your second reading. You should work through the Skills Focus by making annotations, highlighting important concepts, and writing notes or questions in the "Notes" column. Depending on instructions from your teacher, you may need to respond online or use a separate piece of paper to start expanding on your thoughts and ideas.

7 Write

Your study of each selection will end with a writing assignment. For this assignment, you should use your notes, annotations, personal ideas, and answers to both the Think and the Skills Focus questions. Be sure to read the prompt carefully and address each part of it in your writing.

Extended Writing Project and Grammar

This is your opportunity to use genre characteristics and craft to compose meaningful, longer written works exploring the theme of each unit. You will draw information from your readings, research, and own life experiences to complete the assignment.

1 Writing Project

After you have read all of the unit text selections, you will move on to a writing project. Each project will guide you through the process of writing your essay. Student models will provide guidance and help you organize your thoughts. One unit ends with an **Extended Oral Project,** which will give you an opportunity to develop your oral language and communication skills.

2 Writing Process Steps

There are four steps in the writing process: Plan, Draft, Revise, and Edit and Publish. During each step, you will form and shape your writing project, and each lesson's peer review will give you the chance to receive feedback from your peers and teacher.

3 Writing Skills

Each Skill lesson focuses on a specific strategy or technique that you will use during your writing project. Each lesson presents a process for applying the skill to your own work and gives you the opportunity to practice it to improve your writing.

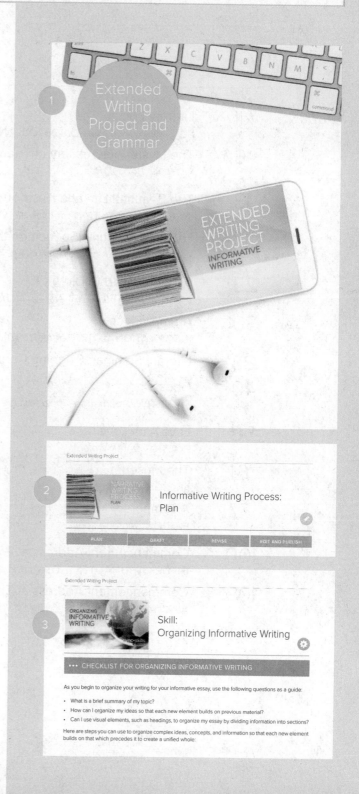

Extended Writing Project

2 Informative Writing Process: Plan

| PLAN | DRAFT | REVISE | EDIT AND PUBLISH |

Extended Writing Project

3 Skill: Organizing Informative Writing

••• CHECKLIST FOR ORGANIZING INFORMATIVE WRITING

As you begin to organize your writing for your informative essay, use the following questions as a guide:

• What is a brief summary of my topic?
• How can I organize my ideas so that each new element builds on previous material?
• Can I use visual elements, such as headings, to organize my essay by dividing information into sections?

Here are steps you can use to organize complex ideas, concepts, and information so that each new element builds on that which precedes it to create a unified whole:

Times of Transition

How are we shaped by change?

> Literary Focus: POSTMODERNISM AND POSTCOLONIALISM

Texts

 PAIRED READINGS

xii   Literary Focus
POSTMODERNISM AND POSTCOLONIALISM

6   The Mysterious Anxiety of Them and Us
FICTION   *Ben Okri*

13   The Beautiful Life and Illustrious Reign of Queen Victoria
INFORMATIONAL TEXT   *John Rusk*

17   Tryst with Destiny (Speech on the Eve of India's Independence)
TALK BACK TEXT   ARGUMENTATIVE TEXT   *Jawaharlal Nehru*

25   I Am Prepared to Die
ARGUMENTATIVE TEXT   *Nelson Mandela*

30   A Small Place
INFORMATIONAL TEXT   *Jamaica Kincaid*

33   Literary Seminar: Ongoing Conversations with the Canon

40   Ghosts
FICTION   *Chimamanda Ngozi Adichie*

58   Love After Love
POETRY   *Derek Walcott*

61   The Museum
FICTION   *Leila Aboulela*

77   A Temporary Matter
FICTION   *Jhumpa Lahiri*

100   Commencement Address at Wellesley College
INFORMATIONAL TEXT   *Chimamanda Ngozi Adichie*

109   Commencement Address at The New School
ARGUMENTATIVE TEXT   *Zadie Smith*

Extended Writing Project and Grammar

126 | Oral Presentation Process: Plan

Organizing an Oral Presentation
Evaluating Sources
Considering Audience and Purpose
Persuasive Techniques

149 | Oral Presentation Process: Draft

Sources and Citations
Communicating Ideas
Reasons and Evidence
Engaging in Discourse

166 | Oral Presentation Process: Revise

Grammar: Parallel Structure
Grammar: Sentence Variety – Openings

173 | Oral Presentation Process: Edit and Publish

 **Talk Back Text** Talk Back Texts are works from a later period that engage with the themes and tropes of the unit's literary focus. Demonstrating that literature is always in conversation, these texts provide dynamic new perspectives to complement the unit's more traditional chronology.

176 | Text Fulfillment through StudySync

Copyright © BookheadEd Learning, LLC

Unit 6: Times of Transition
How are we shaped by change?

LEILA ABOULELA

Leila Aboulela (b. 1964) is a Sudanese writer of short stories and novels. She was born in Cairo, Egypt; raised in Khartoum, Sudan; and has lived much of her adult life in Aberdeen, Scotland. All of her literary works carefully portray the faith and values of her characters, which often feature people who practice Islam and must negotiate ethical dilemmas. Aboulela sees fiction as a "gentle way of passing on information" about Islam to non-Muslim readers.

CHIMAMANDA NGOZI ADICHIE

Chimamanda Ngozi Adichie (b. 1977) writes short stories, novels, and essays, and she splits her time between Nigeria and the United States. Her education has included studies in medicine, communication, political science, African history, and creative writing. Adichie's family lived in the house once owned by the notable Nigerian author Chinua Achebe, a literary figure Adichie credits as her inspiration for becoming a writer.

JAMAICA KINCAID

Jamaica Kincaid (b. 1949) moved from St. John's, Antigua, at the age of sixteen to work as an au pair in New York City and has lived in New York ever since. Kincaid began her writing career as a journalist for a girls' magazine, and as her talent was recognized, she became employed as a staff writer for *The New Yorker*. Critics often struggle to categorize her work, which is by turns both political and personal and like human experience itself: complex, beautiful, and resonant.

JHUMPA LAHIRI

Jhumpa Lahiri (b. 1967) says, "While I am American by virtue of the fact that I was raised in this country, I am Indian thanks to the efforts of two individuals." Lahiri's parents infused her Rhode Island childhood with the language, values, and traditions of their Bengali Indian origins, and the family took frequent trips to Kolkata, the capital of West Bengal. Lahiri's fiction and essays often feature characters who navigate multiple cultural identities, modeled after her own Indian American experience.

JAWAHARLAL NEHRU

Activist, lawyer, and politician Jawaharlal Nehru (1889–1964) was repeatedly imprisoned for civil disobedience in the 1920s and 1930s. A leader of the movement to establish Indian independence from the British administration, Nehru worked closely with Mahatma Gandhi and was recognized as his successor by the end of World War II. Named the first prime minister of India in 1947, Nehru went on to model the new government into a secular republic with democratic values.

NELSON MANDELA

Nelson Mandela (1918–2013) led the emancipation of South Africa from white minority rule and became the country's first democratically elected president in 1994. His election came after he served twenty-seven years in prison on charges of conspiracy to overthrow the South African government. In his 1962 trial testimony, he indicted the state-sanctioned system of apartheid, voicing his opposition to this system of enforced segregation. His reputation grew steadily while he was in prison, and he became an international emblem of freedom and democracy.

BEN OKRI

Ben Okri (b. 1959) spent part of his childhood in London and part in his home of Nigeria, where he experienced the Biafran War firsthand. He was once again living in London when he polished the final draft of *The Famished Road* (1991), which made Okri the youngest ever winner of the Man Booker Prize for Fiction. In prose and in verse, Okri's attention to the music of language and the art of storytelling reflects his lifelong love of literature and deep connection to his Urhobo culture.

ZADIE SMITH

Author Zadie Smith (b. 1975) grew up in London with a Jamaican mother and an English father. She liked to sing, dance, and write from an early age. When she was fourteen, Smith changed the spelling of her first name, Sadie, to its current spelling with a *Z*. Smith pitched her first novel to an agent while she was still in college in Cambridge, England; *White Teeth* (2000) became an instant bestseller. She writes fiction and essays, and works as a professor of creative writing in New York City.

DEREK WALCOTT

The poetry of Derek Walcott (1930–2017) celebrates his Caribbean heritage and interrogates the influence of colonialism. Walcott was raised in the British colony of Saint Lucia in the West Indies, where he trained as a painter and began publishing poems at age fourteen. He later lived in Trinidad, New York City, Boston, and Saint Lucia, working as a poet, playwright, and professor. Walcott defined poetry as a form of survival, cohering the "fragmented memory" of individual and cultural histories.

JOHN RUSK

Born a subject of the British Empire under Queen Victoria, Reverend John Rusk was a citizen of the United States at the time of her death. An effusive admirer of Victoria, Rusk penned a biography intended to memorialize the queen he called "the greatest of all the English monarchs for several centuries, if not for all time." In his account, Rusk pays special attention to Victoria's colonial impact, which he referred to as "the wonderful progress of the British Empire" in the Victorian era.

LITERARY FOCUS:
Postmodernism and Postcolonialism

Introduction

This text offers an introduction to the culture and history that led to the movements of postmodernism and postcolonialism. Postcolonialism developed after the second World War, when British colonies all across the world gained their independence, and those living in the former colonies were left to deal with the violent consequences of years of British rule. Postcolonial writers provided necessary new perspectives in literature from people previously silenced by the dominance of colonial powers. Postmodernism was a response to the end of World War II and the Modernist movement—a kind of rebellion that attempted to expand on literary tradition by exploding it from within.

"Colony by colony, the British Empire was dismantled."

1 You may have heard the word *postmodern* used to describe unusual artwork, literature, music, or even experimental pop and rap stars. Another related term you may be familiar with is *postcolonialism*. Both words represent prominent literary movements of the twentieth and twenty-first centuries. Although you may not yet have a thorough understanding of these movements, more than likely you have noticed that both words have one detail in common: the prefix *post-*, meaning "after." As the word parts signify, **postmodernism** came after Modernism, and **postcolonialism** came after colonialism. Because both movements are reactions to previous historical, cultural, and literary events, it is important to begin by studying what led to these movements, specifically the end of Modernism, British colonialism, and World War II.

British Colonialism

2 During the nineteenth and early twentieth centuries, Britain colonized large portions of the world, with the aim of total control over vast territories. Although the British Empire did build railroads, telegraphs, schools, and hospitals in these territories, colonialism was based on economic exploitation and influenced by racist attitudes. Throughout the British Empire, government administrators and Christian missionaries often came into conflict with the people under colonial rule. Later, writers would describe the devastating effects of British colonialism and the imposition of Christianity on traditional ways of life. One prominent example is Nigerian writer Chinua Achebe's highly acclaimed and influential novel *Things Fall Apart* (1958). It explored the experience of European colonization from the perspective of the Nigerians at a time when most English literature reflected a European viewpoint.

A meeting of British colonial administrators with tribal messengers from the interior in Lagos, Nigeria

The End of the Empire

3   To strengthen its economy after World War II, Britain had to reduce expenses abroad and, therefore, gradually agreed to many colonies' demands for independence. Colony by colony, the British Empire was dismantled. In Asia and Africa, the new nations created from former British colonies faced an array of **formidable** problems, including overpopulation, poverty, and ethnic and religious **strife.** For example, when India and Pakistan became independent in 1947, millions of people fled across new borders, with a majority of Hindus focusing on a newly free India and many Muslims streaming toward Pakistan. In such a chaotic atmosphere of divergent cultures and faiths, mass migration, and new governments, violence ensued, and more than a million people perished. In Africa, many former British colonies achieved independence during the 1950s and 1960s, but their national stability was undermined by ethnic clashes often resulting from arbitrarily drawn borders. When building colonial empires, Britain and other European powers had drawn the boundaries of African nations with little regard to the inhabitants' ethnic diversity or existing territories.

Postmodern and Postcolonial Literature

4   Most literary critics generally accept that the end of World War II marked the end of the Modernist movement and led the way toward postmodernism and postcolonialism. Postmodern literature refers to the literature that emerged after the war in reaction to the previous Modernist movement. In typical Modernist works, authors present a subjective point of view with a focus on one's inner experience and use a stream-of-consciousness narration. Modernist works deal with themes of alienation and uncertain identity. In contrast, postmodernist works focus on the external world and may include an ironic narrator or even multiple narrators offering multiple perspectives on the same event. Themes often reflect collective voices, popular culture, and multicultural experiences.

5   Although it can be difficult to define, postmodernist literature is known for its rebellious approach and willingness to test boundaries. Postmodern literary works reexamine literary tradition. For instance, such works may include a unique combination of multiple genres to comment on postmodern life or demonstrate a self-awareness of the writing form through parody of other texts. One driving idea behind postmodernism is that "everything has already been done," and artists can no longer be completely original. Therefore, postmodernists take a playful approach, drawing inspiration from existing texts, combining forms, and having fun with literary experimentation.

Sotheby's unveils postmodern artist Banksy's newly titled "Love Is in the Bin" on October 12, 2018, in London, England. Originally titled "Girl with Balloon," the canvas passed through a hidden shredder seconds after it sold at Sotheby's London Contemporary Art Evening Sale on October 5, 2018, making it the first artwork in history to have been created live during an auction.

6   Postcolonial literature describes the genre of literature produced by writers of formerly colonized countries. Postcolonial writers describe the struggles of colonization and **decolonization** and often write about themes of identity, racism, and cultural dominance. Their writing challenges many of the assumptions of colonialism, particularly the assertion that European culture was superior and needed to spread to all corners of the world. Many writers from former British colonies, including Chinua Achebe, Wole Soyinka, Derek Walcott, Salman Rushdie, and V. S. Naipaul, address the political and social problems that continue to plague their countries, even after independence.

7   As contemporaneous movements, postcolonial literature shares some similarities with postmodernism, and some postcolonial authors write in a postmodern style. For example, Indian-born author Salman Rushdie has been hailed for his innovative postmodern take on Indian history and independence in his novel *Midnight's Children* (1981). Nigerian poet and novelist Ben Okri is considered one of the foremost African authors of both postmodernism and postcolonialism, and his novel *The Famished Road*, about a quest for identity, won the Booker Prize in 1991.

8   Among the most obvious lasting effects of British colonialism is the large number of English speakers spread throughout the world. Postcolonial writers may have wrestled with the issue of using English, the language of their oppressors, but many choose English because it is so widely spoken and can reach large audiences. Writing in English, these authors reclaim and define their own identities and tell their own stories from their perspectives.

NOTES

9 **Major Concepts**

- **Multiple Perspectives**—Postcolonial writers express different viewpoints about colonization, history, social justice, and culture—and also challenge stereotypes.

- **Decolonization Struggles**—Postcolonial literature criticizes colonial powers but also exposes corruption in postcolonial governments.

- **Self-referentiality**—Postmodernist literature frequently demonstrates self-awareness by referencing other works or even by directly acknowledging the reader or viewer, as when a character might speak directly to the camera about being "watched."

10 **Style and Form**

- Writers of postmodern literature experiment with different literary forms and combines existing forms to create new styles of literature. As a result, writers have created variations and innovations upon traditional forms and themes.

- Postcolonial writers may use established narrative forms and the English language, even though it may not be their native language. This has broadened the scope of English literature in both subject matter and style, adding the voices and experiences of writers from cultures throughout the world.

11 The British Empire may have ended before the age of postmodernism and postcolonialism, but the world of literature has expanded enormously. By adding new perspectives and new voices, literature has become a platform for all narratives and literary experiments.

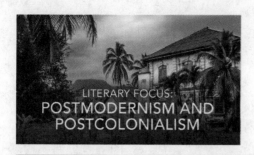

Literary Focus: Postmodernism and Postcolonialism

Read "Literary Focus: Postmodernism and Postcolonialism." After you read, complete the Think Questions below.

 THINK QUESTIONS

1. What were the effects of imperialism? Cite evidence from the text to support your answer.

2. Why does postmodernism rebel against tradition and authority? Cite evidence from the text to support your answer.

3. What effect did British colonialism have on the English language, and why is this important to literature? Cite evidence from the text to support your answers.

4. The word **postmodernism** contains the Latin prefix *post-,* meaning "after." With this information in mind, write your best definition of the word *postmodernism* as it is used in this text. Cite any words or phrases you used to come to your conclusion.

5. Use context clues to determine the meaning of the word **postcolonialism.** Write your best definition here, along with the words and phrases you used to determine the word's meaning. Then check a dictionary to confirm your understanding.

Please note that excerpts and passages in the StudySync® library and this workbook are intended as touchstones to generate interest in an author's work. The excerpts and passages do not substitute for the reading of entire texts, and StudySync® strongly recommends that students seek out and purchase the whole literary or informational work in order to experience it as the author intended. Links to online resellers are available in our digital library. In addition, complete works may be ordered through an authorized reseller by filling out and returning to StudySync® the order form enclosed in this workbook.

Reading & Writing Companion   **5**

The Mysterious Anxiety of Them and Us

FICTION
Ben Okri
2006

Introduction

Ben Okri (b. 1959) is a writer of novels, poetry, short stories, and social commentary from Minna, Nigeria. During his youth, Okri was an avid reader of English literature and an avid listener to his mother's traditional African stories and myths. Okri's writing draws from both influences, often incorporating realism, folktales, and mythology as well as dream logic, or the feeling of being in a dream. In his book *Tales of Freedom*, Okri creates a new form called the "stoku," which he describes as "an amalgam of short story and haiku. It is a story as it inclines towards a flash of a moment, insight, vision or paradox." The invented style can be seen on full display in "The Mysterious Anxiety of Them and Us," a stoku set in a dreamlike atmosphere where an arbitrary distinction engenders an almost surreal tension.

"While we had been eating it had often occurred to me that there was nothing to stop them from sticking knives into our backs."

1 We were in the magnificent grounds of our mysterious host. A feast had been laid out in the open air. There were many of us present. Some were already seated and some were standing behind those seated. In a way there were too many of us for the food served, or it felt like that.

Nigerian poet and novelist Ben Okri

NOTES

Skill:
Story Structure

The author uses vague descriptions to set up the allegory. This is an effective choice because it suggests that the stoku reflects abstract ideas instead of telling about concrete characters, settings, and plot events.

2 There was a moment when it seemed that everyone would rush at the food and we'd have to be **barbaric** and eat with our hands, fighting over the feast laid out on the lovely tables. The moment of tension lasted a long time.

3 Our host did nothing, and said nothing. No one was sure what to do. **Insurrection** brooded in the winds. Then something strange happened. Those who were at table served themselves, and began eating.

4 We ate calmly. My wife was sitting next to me. The food was wonderful.

5 We ate with some awareness of those behind us, who were not eating, and who did not move. They merely watched us eating.

6 Did we who were eating feel guilty? It was a complex feeling. There is no way of resolving it as such. Those who were at table ate. That's it. That's all.

7 We ate a while. Then the people behind us began to murmur. One of them, in a low voice, said:

8 'The first person who offers us some food will receive . . .'

9 I was tempted to offer them some food. But how could I? Where would I start? The situation was impossible. If you turned around, you would see them all. Then your situation would be **polarized.** It would be you and them. But it was never that way to begin with. We were all at the feast. It's just that you were

Please note that excerpts and passages in the StudySync® library and this workbook are intended as touchstones to generate interest in an author's work. The excerpts and passages do not substitute for the reading of entire texts, and StudySync® strongly recommends that students seek out and purchase the whole literary or informational work in order to experience it as the author intended. Links to online resellers are available in our digital library. In addition, complete works may be ordered through an authorized reseller by filling out and returning to StudySync® the order form enclosed in this workbook.

Reading & Writing Companion   7

at the table, and you began to eat. They weren't at table and they didn't eat. They did nothing. They didn't even come over, take a plate, and serve themselves. No one told them, to just stand there watching us eat. They did it to themselves.

10 So to turn around and offer them food would automatically be to see them and treat them as inferior. When in fact they behaved in a manner that made things turn out that way. And so we continued to eat, and ignored the murmurs. Soon we had finished eating. We were satisfied, and took up the invitation to visit other parts of the estate. There was still plenty of food left, as it happened. My wife and I were almost the last to leave the table. As I got up, I looked behind us. I was surprised to see only three people there. Was that all? They had seemed like more, like a crowd. Maybe there had been more of them, but they'd drifted off, given up, or died. While we had been eating it had often occurred to me that there was nothing to stop them from sticking knives into our backs. My wife and I filed out with the others, towards the gardens, in the **sumptuous** grounds of that magnificent estate. It had been a dreamy day of rich sunlight.

Ben Okri, "The Mysterious Anxiety of Them and Us," from *Tales of Freedom*, first published by Rider, an imprint of the Ebury Group, 2009. Copyright © Ben Okri 2009. Reproduced by permission of Ben Okri c/o Georgina Capel Associates Ltd., 29 Wardour Street, London, W1D 6PS.

First Read

Read "The Mysterious Anxiety of Them and Us." After you read, complete the Think Questions below.

 THINK QUESTIONS

1. In the middle of paragraph 3, the narrator says, "Then something strange happened." Citing evidence from the text, explain what happened. How does what occurred affect the narrator's feelings?

2. In paragraph 6, the narrator asks, "Did we who were eating feel guilty?" How does he respond to his own question? What does the way he answers tell you about him? Use examples from the text to support your answer.

3. How did you react to the last sentence, "It had been a dreamy day of rich sunlight"? Do you think it is consistent with the tone of the rest of the text? Use evidence from the text to support your answer.

4. What is the meaning of the word **insurrection** as it is used in the text? Write your best definition here, along with a brief explanation of how you arrived at its meaning.

5. Use context clues to determine the meaning of the word **sumptuous** as it is used in "The Mysterious Anxiety of Them and Us." Write your definition of *sumptuous* here, along with those words or phrases from the text you used to define it. Then check a dictionary to confirm your understanding.

Please note that excerpts and passages in the StudySync® library and this workbook are intended as touchstones to generate interest in an author's work. The excerpts and passages do not substitute for the reading of entire texts, and StudySync® strongly recommends that students seek out and purchase the whole literary or informational work in order to experience it as the author intended. Links to online resellers are available in our digital library. In addition, complete works may be ordered through an authorized reseller by filling out and returning to StudySync® the order form enclosed in this workbook.

Reading & Writing Companion

9

Skill:
Story Structure

Use the Checklist to analyze Story Structure in "The Mysterious Anxiety of Them and Us." Refer to the sample student annotations about Story Structure in the text.

••• CHECKLIST FOR STORY STRUCTURE

In order to identify the choices an author makes when structuring specific parts of a text, note the following:

✓ the choices an author makes to organize specific parts of a text such as where to begin and end a story, or whether the ending should be tragic, comic, or inconclusive

✓ the author's use of any literary devices, such as:

  • pacing: how quickly or slowly the events of a story unfold

  • allegory: a story or poem that conveys a hidden meaning that is usually moral or political

✓ how the overall structure of the text contributes to its meaning as well as its aesthetic impact, such as

  • an allegorical story structure

  • the creation of suspense through the use of pacing

To analyze how an author's choices concerning how to structure specific parts of a text contribute to its overall structure and meaning as well as its aesthetic impact, consider the following questions:

✓ How does the author structure the text overall? How does the author structure specific parts of the text?

✓ Does the author incorporate literary elements such as allegory? How do these elements affect the overall text structure and the aesthetic impact of the text?

✓ What is the literal or everyday meaning of the narrative? What would the allegorical meaning of the narrative be? How do the characters, setting, and plot work together to convey this message?

Copyright © BookheadEd Learning, LLC

Skill:
Story Structure

Reread paragraph 9 of "The Mysterious Anxiety of Them and Us." Then use the Checklist on the previous page to answer the multiple-choice questions below.

↻ YOUR TURN

1. What is the literal meaning of paragraph 9?

   ○ A. The people standing behind will eat after the people sitting are done.

   ○ B. The host created this situation as a test to see what the narrator would do.

   ○ C. The narrator thinks the best thing to do in this situation is not turn around.

   ○ D. The fact that some get more than others is universal and impossible to change.

2. What is the symbolic meaning of paragraph 9?

   ○ A. People need to take responsibility for their own life and well-being.

   ○ B. The events that happened at the feast could happen to anyone in real life.

   ○ C. The people standing behind have to wait their turn to eat because they arrived late.

   ○ D. Wealthy people avoid thinking about the poor because they do not want to feel guilty.

3. The language Okri uses to develop allegory in this paragraph is effective because it—

   ○ A. suggests that people are not responsible for their own actions.

   ○ B. reflects the way wealthy people rationalize their actions.

   ○ C. describes explicit conflict between two social groups.

   ○ D. emphasizes the struggles of people living in poverty.

Please note that excerpts and passages in the StudySync® library and this workbook are intended as touchstones to generate interest in an author's work. The excerpts and passages do not substitute for the reading of entire texts, and StudySync® strongly recommends that students seek out and purchase the whole literary or informational work in order to experience it as the author intended. Links to online resellers are available in our digital library. In addition, complete works may be ordered through an authorized reseller by filling out and returning to StudySync® the order form enclosed in this workbook.

Reading & Writing
Companion

11

THE MYSTERIOUS ANXIETY
OF THEM AND US

Close Read

Reread "The Mysterious Anxiety of Them and Us." As you reread, complete the Skills Focus questions below. Then use your answers and annotations from the questions to help you complete the Write activity.

SKILLS FOCUS

1. Identify a detail that is suggestive of a hidden meaning or abstract idea, and explain how it effectively contributes to the story's allegorical structure.

2. Identify an example of simple, plain writing in the text, and explain how the author's choice to use this diction and syntax contributes to the effectiveness of the allegory.

3. Identify a sentence that inspires readers to have an emotional response. Explain how this author's use of language effectively shapes the reader's perceptions of the narrator or events.

4. Re-read the final paragraph of the story. Using context clues, determine the part of speech and possible meaning of the word *magnificent*. Then, highlight the word and in your annotation explain why the author's choice to repeat this word at the beginning and end of the story is important in the final impact of the story.

5. Throughout this allegorical short story, the narrator describes changes in thinking and in feeling about this strange situation. Highlight two instances of these changes, and in your annotation describe the impact they have on you, the reader.

WRITE

LITERARY ANALYSIS: This work is written in an allegorical, dreamlike structure with little explanation of what is happening and why. What do you think is the "mysterious anxiety"? Who do you think are the "them and us"? Write a brief literary analysis that explains the events and the theme as you see them, which may not be the way your classmates see them. Tell what you think of the narrator, and point out connections between the text and the real world. Support your ideas with textual evidence when you can.

Copyright © BookheadEd Learning, LLC

The Beautiful Life and Illustrious Reign of Queen Victoria

INFORMATIONAL TEXT

John Rusk

1901

Introduction

On January 1, 1877, Victoria was crowned Empress of India. While British influence through the East India Company dates back to 1612, the British Crown did not directly take control of the country until 1858. Not satisfied with ruling multiple territories on paper, the British Parliament declared that Victoria was no longer just a queen but an empress. In this text, published nearly 30 years later, John Rusk (1849–1910) provides an exuberant account of Queen Victoria's glittering coronation ceremony and her ongoing interest in India. Rusk's rosy view of Britain's growing empire reflects a nostalgic look back at Queen Victoria's reign from the year of her death.

"At the Imperial camp . . . where the mutiny had raged the fiercest, Her Majesty was proclaimed Empress of India."

NOTES

1   Far away in sunny India was enacted, on January 1, 1877, a scene the most brilliant and unique of any connected with the glorious reign of Victoria. At the Imperial camp,[1] outside the walls of Delhi, where the mutiny had raged the fiercest, Her Majesty was proclaimed Empress of India. On a throne of oriental splendor, above which was a portrait of the Empress, sat Lord Lytton, her Viceroy, the Governors, Lieutenants, State officials and the Maharajahs, Rajahs, Nabobs and Princes, with their glittering retinues grouped around him. Behind rose the vast amphitheatre, filled with foreign ambassadors and notables; around was the concourse of spectators and a brilliant array of fifteen thousand troops, while to complete the gorgeous scene the whole assemblage was surrounded by an unbroken chain of elephants decked with gay trappings. After the proclamation had been made with all the pomp of heraldry, the Viceroy presented to each of the feudatory Princes the gift of the Empress, a magnificent standard designed by Her Majesty. The standards were ornamented with the sacred water lily of India, spreading palms of the East, and the rose of England, it being the desire of the Empress to indicate that as the rose and lily intertwined beneath the spreading palm, so was the welfare of India to become one with that of her older dominions; and the motto, "Heaven's light our guide," illustrated the spirit in which she desired to govern the enormous empire of which she ever fondly spoke as "a bright jewel in her crown." Most noticeable in the brilliant gathering was the Begum of Bhopal, a lady Knight of the Most Noble Order of Queen Victoria. There was nothing to be seen of the lady save a bundle of floating azure silk, which indicated that she was inside, and upon the place where the left shoulder was supposed to be emblazoned the shield of the Star of India.

. . .

2   The keenest interest was always shown by the Queen in the condition of Hindoo[2] women. It was with her heartfelt thankfulness that she saw the barbarous suttee[3] abolished, and it was her influence which inspired the

---

1. **Imperial camp** the military camp for the British Indian Army
2. **Hindoo** a follower of the Hindu religion
3. **suttee** an old practice in India in which a widow would throw herself onto the funeral pyre of her dead husband

rapid spread of Zenana[4] work. In July, 1881, she received at Windsor Miss Beilby, a medical missionary from India; and after listening to her account of the sufferings of Hindoo women, in time of illness, for need of doctors, the Queen turned to her ladies and said, "We had no idea that things were as bad as this." Miss Beilby then took from a locket which she wore round her neck a folded piece of paper containing a message to Her Majesty from the Maharanee of Poonah. "The women of India suffer when they are sick," was the burden of the dark-eyed Queen's appeal. The Empress returned her a message of sympathy and help, and to the women of England the Queen said, "We desire it to be generally known that we sympathize with every effort made to relieve the suffering of the state of women in India"; and when Lord Dufferin went out as Governor-General, she **commissioned** Lady Dufferin to establish a permanent fund for providing qualified women doctors for work in India. Her Majesty continued to take the greatest interest in this work, and was in constant communication with the Viceroy's wife regarding its further organization and **extension,** up to the time of her death.

3   No opportunity was lost by Her Majesty to show her interest in her Indian Empire, and doubtless had the Prince Consort been spared she would have made progress through the country. This was done in her stead by the Prince of Wales in 1875–6, and it was while he was making the tour that Lord Beaconsfield introduced the Royal Titles Bill into Parliament, **conferring** upon the Queen the title of Empress of India, a distinction regarded by John Bull as superfluous to a Crown the most distinguished in the world; but Her Majesty personally desired it, not, as gossip affirmed, because of the advent at Court of her second son's Imperial bride, but as a means of **binding** her Indian subjects to her in a closer manner. It is said that she showed more interest in the Indian Court of the Colonial Exhibition, 1886, than in any other, and at each of her visits chatted freely with the native workmen. When the Indian delegates to the Exhibition first saw their Empress, a homely-looking lady in a black silk gown, they expressed disappointment, having expected to see her decked out in the pomp and circumstance of a mighty **potentate.** "But, after all," said they, "what a great power the Queen must wield when she can command such an array of illustrious personages to attend upon her, while she appears as the most simple of all the Court." In later years Her Majesty had Indian servants in native dress as personal attendants; she was also an assiduous student of Hindustani,[5] being able to speak and write in that language; and her favorite State jewel was the priceless Koh-i-noor, about which hangs a tale. When it came into the possession of the East India Company, in 1850, it was handed at a Board meeting to John Lawrence (afterwards Lord Lawrence, the Viceroy) for safe keeping. The precious diamond was laid amongst folds of linen in a small box, and Lord Lawrence

4. **Zenana** a section of the house designated for women in order to seclude them from men
5. **Hindustani** a family of dialects spoken in northern India

Reading & Writing
Companion   **15**

NOTES

slipped it into his waistcoat pocket and forgot all about it until some days later it was suggested that he should forward it to the Queen. One can imagine his consternation when he rushed to his house to see if it was to be found. "Have you seen a small box in one of my waistcoat pockets?" he asked breathlessly of his servant. "Yes, sahib," was the reply. "I found it and put it in one of your boxes." "Bring it here and open it, and see what it contains," said his master. "There is nothing in it, sahib, but a bit of glass," the man replied in wonderment. The "bit of glass" was in due course despatched to the Queen, whose crown it was to adorn; but she preferred to wear it on occasions as a magnificent brooch in the centre of her bodice. The cutting of the diamond was personally superintended by the Prince Consort.

✏ WRITE

EXPLANATORY: *The Beautiful Life and Illustrious Reign of Queen Victoria* was written in 1901, the year of Queen Victoria's death, and presents the queen as she commences her role as Empress of India. How does the text depict this event? Explain the historical context in which the text was written and how it may have influenced the way the queen and British imperialism are portrayed. Include the most relevant evidence from the text to support your response.

Tryst with Destiny
(Speech on the Eve of India's Independence)

ARGUMENTATIVE TEXT
Jawaharlal Nehru
1947

Introduction

This speech, given to announce India's independence from almost 200 years of British rule, was delivered to Parliament by Jawaharlal Nehru (1889–1964), the man who would become India's first prime minister. After studying law at Cambridge, Nehru returned to India, where he eventually became Mohandas Gandhi's successor. Nehru's daughter, Indira Gandhi, who later became prime minister of India, was the first and only woman to hold the post. In this triumphant address, Jawaharlal Nehru celebrates Indian victory but also earnestly urges his fellow patriots to consider the kind of future they intend to forge for their country.

"We end today a period of ill fortune and India discovers herself again."

NOTES

Skill:
Rhetoric

Nehru directly addresses the audience, using the pronoun we to show a shared interest in India's independence. He also uses figurative language to persuade the audience to recognize the importance of the moment.

I

1 Long years ago we made a tryst with destiny, and now the time comes when we shall redeem our pledge, not wholly or in full measure, but very substantially. At the stroke of the midnight hour, when the world sleeps, India will awake to life and freedom. A moment comes, which comes but rarely in history, when we step out from the old to the new, when an age ends, and when the soul of a nation, long suppressed, finds **utterance.** It is fitting that at this solemn moment we take the pledge of dedication to the service of India and her people and to the still larger cause of humanity.

Schoolchildren in front of Red Fort on the 72nd Independence Day, on August 15, 2018, in New Delhi, India

2 At the dawn of history India started on her unending quest, and trackless centuries are filled with her striving and the grandeur of her success and her failures. Through good and ill fortune alike she has never lost sight of that quest or forgotten the ideals which gave her strength. We end today a period of ill fortune and India discovers herself again. The achievement we celebrate today is but a step, an opening of opportunity, to the greater triumphs and achievements that await us. Are we brave enough and wise enough to grasp this opportunity and accept the challenge of the future?

3 Freedom and power bring responsibility. The responsibility rests upon this Assembly, a **sovereign** body representing the sovereign people of India. Before the birth of freedom we have endured all the pains of labour and our hearts are heavy with the memory of this sorrow. Some of those pains continue even now. Nevertheless, the past is over and it is the future that beckons to us now.

4   That future is not one of ease or resting but of **incessant** striving so that we may fulfil the pledges we have so often taken and the one we shall take today. The service of India means the service of the millions who suffer. It means the ending of poverty and **ignorance** and disease and inequality of opportunity. The ambition of the greatest man of our generation has been to wipe every tear from every eye. That may be beyond us, but as long as there are tears and suffering, so long our work will not be over.

5   And so we have to labour and to work, and work hard, to give reality to our dreams. Those dreams are for India, but they are also for the world, for all the nations and peoples are too closely knit together today for any one of them to imagine that it can live apart. Peace has been said to be indivisible; so is freedom, so is prosperity now, and so also is disaster in this One World that can no longer be split into isolated fragments.

6   To the people of India, whose representatives we are, we make an appeal to join us with faith and confidence in this great adventure. This is no time for petty and destructive criticism, no time for ill-will or blaming others. We have to build the noble mansion of free India where all her children may dwell.

    II

7   The appointed day has come—the day appointed by destiny—and India stands forth again, after long slumber and struggle, awake, vital, free and independent. The past clings on to us still in some measure and we have to do much before we redeem the pledges we have so often taken. Yet the turning-point is past, and history begins anew for us, the history which we shall live and act and others will write about.

8   It is a fateful moment for us in India, for all Asia and for the world. A new star rises, the star of freedom in the East, a new hope comes into being, a vision long cherished materializes. May the star never set and that hope never be betrayed!

9   We rejoice in that freedom, even though clouds surround us, and many of our people are sorrowstricken and difficult problems encompass us. But freedom brings responsibilities and burdens and we have to face them in the spirit of a free and disciplined people.

10 On this day our first thoughts go to the architect of this freedom, the Father of our Nation [Gandhi], who, embodying the old spirit of India, held aloft the torch of freedom and lighted up the darkness that surrounded us. We have often been unworthy followers of his and have strayed from his message, but not only we but succeeding generations will remember this message and bear the imprint in their hearts of this great son of India, magnificent in his

Please note that excerpts and passages in the StudySync® library and this workbook are intended as touchstones to generate interest in an author's work. The excerpts and passages do not substitute for the reading of entire texts, and StudySync® strongly recommends that students seek out and purchase the whole literary or informational work in order to experience it as the author intended. Links to online resellers are available in our digital library. In addition, complete works may be ordered through an authorized reseller by filling out and returning to StudySync® the order form enclosed in this workbook.

Reading & Writing Companion   19

NOTES

faith and strength and courage and humility. We shall never allow that torch of freedom to be blown out, however high the wind or stormy the tempest.

11 Our next thoughts must be of the unknown volunteers and soldiers of freedom who, without praise or reward, have served India even unto death.

12 We think also of our brothers and sisters who have been cut off from us by political boundaries and who unhappily cannot share at present in the freedom that has come. They are of us and will remain of us whatever may happen, and we shall be sharers in their good [or] ill fortune alike.

13 The future beckons to us. Whither do we go and what shall be our endeavour? To bring freedom and opportunity to the common man, to the peasants and workers of India; to fight and end poverty and ignorance and disease; to build up a prosperous, democratic and progressive nation, and to create social, economic and political institutions which will ensure justice and fullness of life to every man and woman.

14 We have hard work ahead. There is no resting for any one of us till we redeem our pledge in full, till we make all the people of India what destiny intended them to be. We are citizens of a great country on the verge of bold advance, and we have to live up to that high standard. All of us, to whatever religion we may belong, are equally the children of India with equal rights, privileges and obligations. We cannot encourage communalism[1] or narrow-mindedness, for no nation can be great whose people are narrow in thought or in action.

15 To the nations and peoples of the world we send greetings and pledge ourselves to cooperate with them in furthering peace, freedom and democracy.

16 And to India, our much-loved motherland, the ancient, the eternal and the ever-new, we pay our **reverent** homage and we bind ourselves afresh to her service.

17 JAI HIND.

---

1. **communalism** a system that encourages loyalty to narrower communities or identities over an allegiance to society writ large

First Read

Read "Tryst with Destiny (Speech on the Eve of India's Independence)." After you read, complete the Think Questions below.

 THINK QUESTIONS

1. What kind of future does Nehru envision for India? Be specific and provide evidence from the text to support your response.

2. Who is "the greatest man of our generation" that Nehru refers to in his speech? What values did he instill that India's citizens should bring forth into their new nation? Be sure to use evidence from the text to back up your assertions.

3. Why does Nehru insist that India's future must not be "one of ease or resting"? Why is this so important? Be sure to use evidence from the speech to support your response.

4. Use context clues to determine the meaning of the word **incessant.** Write your definition of *incessant,* along with any words or phrases from the text you used to come to your conclusion. Finally, check an online or print dictionary to confirm your understanding.

5. The word **reverent** stems from the Latin word *revereri,* which means to "stand in awe of." With this in mind, write your best definition of *reverent* as it is used in the text. Note any words or phrases you used to determine its meaning.

Please note that excerpts and passages in the StudySync® library and this workbook are intended as touchstones to generate interest in an author's work. The excerpts and passages do not substitute for the reading of entire texts, and StudySync® strongly recommends that students seek out and purchase the whole literary or informational work in order to experience it as the author intended. Links to online resellers are available in our digital library. In addition, complete works may be ordered through an authorized reseller by filling out and returning to StudySync® the order form enclosed in this workbook.

Reading & Writing Companion **21**

Skill:
Rhetoric

Use the Checklist to analyze Rhetoric in "Tryst with Destiny (Speech on the Eve of India's Independence)." Refer to the sample student annotations about Rhetoric in the text.

••• CHECKLIST FOR RHETORIC

To analyze rhetoric in a text, note the following:

✓ the purpose of the text

✓ details and statements that identify the author's point of view or purpose

✓ when the author uses rhetoric to advance their point of view or purpose. Rhetoric is the way in which a writer phrases, or constructs, what they want to say. Writers use many different kinds of rhetorical devices, and the style they employ can contribute to the power, persuasiveness, or beauty of the text. Look for:

- an author's use of sensory language

- words that appeal to the senses can create a vivid picture in the minds of readers and listeners, and persuade them to accept a specific point of view

- a specific style, such as the use of assonance or the repetition of certain words can be used to create catchphrases, something that can be widely or repeatedly used and is easily remembered

- when the author's use of rhetoric is particularly effective

To determine an author's point of view or purpose in a text in which the rhetoric is particularly effective, consider the following questions:

✓ Which rhetorical devices can you identify in the text?

✓ How does this writer or speaker use rhetorical devices to persuade an audience?

✓ Do the rhetorical devices work to make the argument or position sound? Why or why not?

✓ How does the use of rhetorical devices affect the way the text is read and understood? In what way are the rhetorical devices particularly effective?

Copyright © Bookheaded Learning, LLC

Skill:
Rhetoric

Reread paragraphs 8–10 from "Tryst with Destiny (Speech on the Eve of India's Independence)." Then use the Checklist on the previous page to answer the multiple-choice questions below.

⟳ YOUR TURN

1. Nehru's metaphor comparing India's freedom to a new star suggests that—

   ○ A. India's freedom was completely unexpected.

   ○ B. India's freedom was fragile and not expected to last.

   ○ C. India's freedom was a sign of hope to inspire the world.

   ○ D. India's freedom was realized through good luck and fate.

2. What effect does the imagery of light and darkness have on the speech?

   ○ A. It reveals that light and darkness always exist together.

   ○ B. It suggests a different message from the rest of the speech.

   ○ C. It shows that India's leader Gandhi had positive and negative qualities.

   ○ D. It reinforces that light represents freedom while darkness represents tyranny.

Please note that excerpts and passages in the StudySync® library and this workbook are intended as touchstones to generate interest in an author's work. The excerpts and passages do not substitute for the reading of entire texts, and StudySync® strongly recommends that students seek out and purchase the whole literary or informational work in order to experience it as the author intended. Links to online resellers are available in our digital library. In addition, complete works may be ordered through an authorized reseller by filling out and returning to StudySync® the order form enclosed in this workbook.

Reading & Writing Companion   23

Close Read

Reread "Tryst with Destiny." As you reread, complete the Skills Focus questions below. Then use your answers and annotations from the questions to help you complete the Write activity.

1. Identify an example of problem-and-solution text structure in "Tryst with Destiny (Speech on the Eve of India's Independence)," and explain how the author uses this text structure to achieve his purpose.

2. Highlight a passage in the speech where the author's purpose is to inspire people. Write a sentence that explains how the author achieves this purpose.

3. Highlight a word or phrase that generates an emotional response. Explain how this use of language shapes the audience's perceptions and how it contributes to the author's purpose.

4. *The Beautiful Life and Illustrious Reign of Queen Victoria* presents a glorified view of British imperialism in India. Identify moments in Nehru's speech in which he presents a different view of India and its relationship with Britain, and explain the significance of those arguments.

✏ WRITE

RHETORICAL ANALYSIS: John Rusk and Jawaharlal Nehru approach the beginning and end of British Colonial India from very different perspectives. Consider the way Nehru responds to the legacy of colonialism in India. Identify the audience of Nehru's speech and what the speaker wants from them. How do rhetorical devices such as personification and repetition likely affect the crowd's emotions and work together to create a speech that is memorable and important?

I Am Prepared to Die

ARGUMENTATIVE TEXT
Nelson Mandela
1964

Introduction

In 1962, political leader Nelson Mandela (1918–2013) was arrested for participating in a conspiracy to overthrow the South African government. Nearly two years later, Mandela was sentenced to life in prison. In this excerpt from his trial testimony in Rivonia, Mandela indicts the state-sanctioned system of apartheid, explaining why he and several others plotted acts of guerilla warfare against his segregated nation. After serving 27 years in prison, Mandela became the first democratically elected president of South Africa. Many South Africans refer to him as *Madiba*, or "father of the nation."

"During my lifetime I have dedicated myself to this struggle of the African people."

from Nelson Mandela's Statement at the Rivonia Trial,[1] 1964

1   South Africa is the richest country in Africa, and could be one of the richest countries in the world. But it is a land of extremes and remarkable **contrasts.** The whites enjoy what may well be the highest standard of living in the world, whilst Africans live in poverty and misery. Forty percent of the Africans live in hopelessly overcrowded and, in some cases, drought-stricken reserves, where soil erosion and the overworking of the soil makes it impossible for them to live properly off the land. Thirty percent are labourers, labour tenants,[2] and squatters on white farms and work and live under conditions similar to those of the serfs[3] of the Middle Ages. The other thirty percent live in towns where they have developed economic and social habits which bring them closer in many respects to white standards. Yet most Africans, even in this group, are impoverished by low incomes and the high cost of living.

2   The highest-paid and the most **prosperous** section of urban African life is in Johannesburg. Yet their actual position is desperate. The latest figures were given on the 25th of March 1964 by Mr. Carr, Manager of the Johannesburg Non-European Affairs Department. The poverty datum line for the average African family in Johannesburg, according to Mr. Carr's department, is R42.84 per month. He showed that the average monthly wage is R32.24 and that forty-six percent of all African families in Johannesburg do not earn enough to keep them going.

3   Poverty goes hand in hand with **malnutrition** and disease. The incidence of malnutrition and deficiency diseases is very high amongst Africans. Tuberculosis, pellagra, kwashiorkor, gastroenteritis, and scurvy bring death and destruction of health. The incidence of infant mortality is one of the highest in the world. According to the Medical Officer of Health for Pretoria, it is estimated that tuberculosis kills forty people a day, almost all Africans, and

1. **Rivonia Trial** the criminal trial where Nelson Mandela and others were convicted of sabotage and sentenced to life in prison
2. **labour tenant** a farm worker who is unpaid, except for free residence on that farm and a portion of the land to work for themselves
3. **serf** a member of the most servile class, usually bound to physical labor

in 1961 there were 58,491 new cases reported. These diseases, My Lord, not only destroy the vital organs of the body, but they result in retarded mental conditions and lack of initiative, and reduce powers of concentration. The secondary results of such conditions affect the whole community and the standard of work performed by Africans.

4   The complaint of Africans, however, is not only that they are poor and whites are rich, but that the laws which are made by the whites are designed to preserve this situation.

5   There are two ways to break out of poverty. The first is by formal education, and the second is by the worker acquiring a greater skill at his work and thus higher wages. As far as Africans are concerned, both these avenues of advancement are deliberately **curtailed** by legislation.

6   I ask the Court to remember that the present Government has always sought to **hamper** Africans in their search for education. One of their early acts, after coming into power, was to stop subsidies for African school feeding. Many African children who attended schools depended on this supplement to their diet. This was a cruel act.

7   There is compulsory education for all white children at virtually no cost to their parents, be they rich or poor. Similar facilities are not provided for the African children, though there are some who receive such assistance. African children, however, generally have to pay more for their schooling than whites. According to figures quoted by the South African Institute of Race Relations in its 1963 journal, approximately forty percent of African children in the age group between seven and fourteen do not attend school. For those who do attend school, the standards are vastly different from those afforded to white children. In 1960-61 the per capita[4] Government spending on African students at State-aided schools was estimated at R12.46. In the same years, the per capita spending on white children in the Cape Province (which are the only figures available to me) was R144.57. Although there are no figures available to me, it can be stated, without doubt, that the white children on whom R144.57 per head was being spent all came from wealthier homes than African children on whom R12.46 per head was being spent.

8   The quality of education is also different. According to the Bantu Educational Journal, only 5,660 African children in the whole of South Africa passed their Junior Certificate in 1962, and in that year only 362 passed matric.[5] This is presumably consistent with the policy of Bantu Education about which the present Prime Minister said, during the debate on the Bantu Education Bill in 1953 when he was Minister of Native Affairs:

---

4. **per capita** for each person
5. **matric** the requirements for university admission

"When I have control of Native Education I will reform it so that Natives will be taught from childhood to realise that equality with Europeans is not for them. People who believe in equality are not desirable teachers for Natives. When my Department controls Native education it will know for what class of higher education a Native is fitted, and whether he will have a chance in life to use his knowledge."

9   The other main obstacle to the economic advancement of the African is the Industrial Colour Bar under which all the better paid, better jobs of industry are reserved for whites only. Moreover, Africans in the unskilled and semi-skilled occupations which are open to them are not allowed to form trade unions which have recognition under the Industrial Conciliation Act. This means that strikes of African workers are illegal, and that they are denied the right of collective bargaining which is permitted to the better-paid white workers. The discrimination in the policy of successive South African Governments towards African workers is demonstrated by the so-called 'civilized labour policy' under which sheltered, unskilled Government jobs are found for those white workers who cannot make the grade in industry, at wages far, which far exceed the earnings of the average African employee in industry.

10   The Government often answers its critics by saying that Africans in South Africa are economically better off than the inhabitants of the other countries in Africa. I do not know whether this statement is true and doubt whether any comparison can be made without having regard to the cost-of-living index in such countries. But even if it is true, as far as African people are concerned, it is irrelevant. Our complaint is not that we are poor by comparison with people in other countries, but that we are poor by comparison with white people in our own country, and that we are prevented by legislation from altering this imbalance.

11   The lack of human dignity experienced by Africans is the direct result of the policy of white supremacy. White supremacy **implies** black inferiority. Legislation designed to preserve white supremacy entrenches this notion. Menial tasks in South Africa are invariably performed by Africans. When anything has to be carried or cleaned the white man will look around for an African to do it for him, whether the African is employed by him or not. Because of this sort of attitude, whites tend to regard Africans as a separate breed. They do not look upon them as people with families of their own; they do not realise that we have emotions—that we fall in love like white people do; that we want to be with our wives and children like white people want to be with theirs; that we want to earn money, enough money to support our families properly, to feed and clothe them and send them to school. And what 'house-boy' or 'garden-boy' or labourer can ever hope to do this?

. . .

12 During my lifetime I have dedicated myself to this struggle of the African people. I have fought against white domination, and I have fought against black domination. I have cherished the ideal of a democratic and free society in which all persons live together in harmony and with equal opportunities. It is an ideal which I hope to live for and to achieve. But if needs be, it is an ideal for which I am prepared to die.

Prisoners raising their fists in protest from inside a prison car carrying eight men, including Nelson Mandela, after being sentenced to life imprisonment for conspiracy, sabotage and treason, 1964

✎ WRITE

RHETORICAL ANALYSIS: The ancient Greek philosopher Aristotle wrote the *Rhetoric,* one of the most famous works on the art of persuasion. In the treatise, he outlines the main rhetorical appeals to an audience: ethos (author credibility), pathos (emotions), and logos (logic and reasoning). How does Mandela use these appeals to advance his argument? Use specific textual evidence to support your response.

Please note that excerpts and passages in the StudySync® library and this workbook are intended as touchstones to generate interest in an author's work. The excerpts and passages do not substitute for the reading of entire texts, and StudySync® strongly recommends that students seek out and purchase the whole literary or informational work in order to experience it as the author intended. Links to online resellers are available in our digital library. In addition, complete works may be ordered through an authorized reseller by filling out and returning to StudySync® the order form enclosed in this workbook.

Reading & Writing Companion   29

A Small Place

INFORMATIONAL TEXT
Jamaica Kincaid
1988

Introduction

Jamaica Kincaid (b. 1949) was born Elaine Potter Richardson on the Caribbean island of Antigua. Raised in poverty, she was sent at the age of 17 to work as an au pair in New York. There, she began her writing career, eventually penning short fiction featured in publications like the *Paris Review* and becoming a long-tenured staff writer at the *New Yorker*. Much of her writing centers on themes of colonial legacy, racism, class, and power dynamics. These themes are well evident in *A Small Place,* a work of creative nonfiction that draws heavily on the author's experiences growing up in Antigua.

"You will have to accept that this is mostly your fault."

1   Have you ever wondered to yourself why it is that all people like me seem to have learned from you is how to imprison and murder each other, how to govern badly, and how to take the wealth of our country and place it in Swiss bank accounts?[1] Have you ever wondered why it is that all we seem to have learned from you is how to corrupt our societies and how to be **tyrants**? You will have to accept that this is mostly your fault. Let me just show you how you looked to us. You came. You took things that were not yours, and you did not even, for appearances' sake, ask first. You could have said, "May I have this, please?" and even though it would have been clear to everybody that a yes or no from us would have been of no consequence you might have looked so much better. Believe me, it would have gone a long way. I would have had to admit that at least you were polite. You murdered people. You imprisoned people. You robbed people. You opened your own banks and you put our money in them. The accounts were in your name. The banks were in your name. There must have been some good people among you, but they stayed home. And that is the point. That is why they are good. They stayed home. But still, when you think about it, you must be a little sad. The people like me, finally, after years and years of agitation, made deeply moving and **eloquent** speeches against the wrongness of your domination over us, and then finally, after the mutilated bodies of you, your wife, and your children were found in your beautiful and spacious bungalow[2] at the edge of your rubber plantation[3]— found by one of your many house servants (none of it was ever yours; it was never, ever yours)—you say to me, "Well, I wash my hands of all of you, I am leaving now," and you leave, and from afar you watch as we do to ourselves the very things you used to do to us. And you might feel that there was more to you than that, you might feel that you had understood the meaning of the Age of Enlightenment (though, as far as I can see, it had done you very little good); you loved knowledge, and wherever you went you made sure to build a school, a library (yes, and in both of these places you distorted or erased my history and glorified your own). But then again, perhaps as you observe

1. **Swiss bank accounts** authorities have repeatedly found Swiss bank accounts held by criminal enterprises or tax evaders to take advantage of the country's financial secrecy laws
2. **bungalow** a simple, small house or cottage, usually one story
3. **rubber plantation** a large-scale farm for growing and harvesting rubber from trees

NOTES

the **debacle** in which I now exist, the utter ruin that I say is my life, perhaps you are remembering that you had always felt people like me cannot run things, people like me will never grasp the idea of Gross National Product,[4] people like me will never be able to take command of the thing the most simpleminded among you can master, people like me will never understand the notion of rule by law, people like me cannot really think in **abstractions,** people like me cannot be **objective,** we make everything so personal. You will forget your part in the whole setup, that bureaucracy is one of your inventions, that Gross National Product is one of your inventions, and all the laws that you know mysteriously favour you. Do you know why people like me are shy about being capitalists? Well, it's because we, for as long as we have known you, *were* capital, like bales of cotton and sacks of sugar, and you were the commanding, cruel capitalists, and the memory of this is so strong, the experience is so recent, that we can't quite bring ourselves to embrace this idea that you think so much of.

Excerpted from *A Small Place* by Jamaica Kincaid, published by Farrar, Straus & Giroux.

✏ WRITE

CORRESPONDENCE: Like Jamaica Kincaid, write a letter protesting a great wrong done to you or a group to which you belong. Direct the letter to the person you hold responsible, such as a government official, a business executive, a criminal, or a bully. You might copy Kincaid's acid tone or other techniques she uses to make her message effective, or you might deliberately choose different techniques if you think they work better. Be sure your ideas flow logically. You want to make it clear to the person you are writing to why he or she is in the wrong.

---

4. **Gross National Product** the total economic value generated by a country in one year

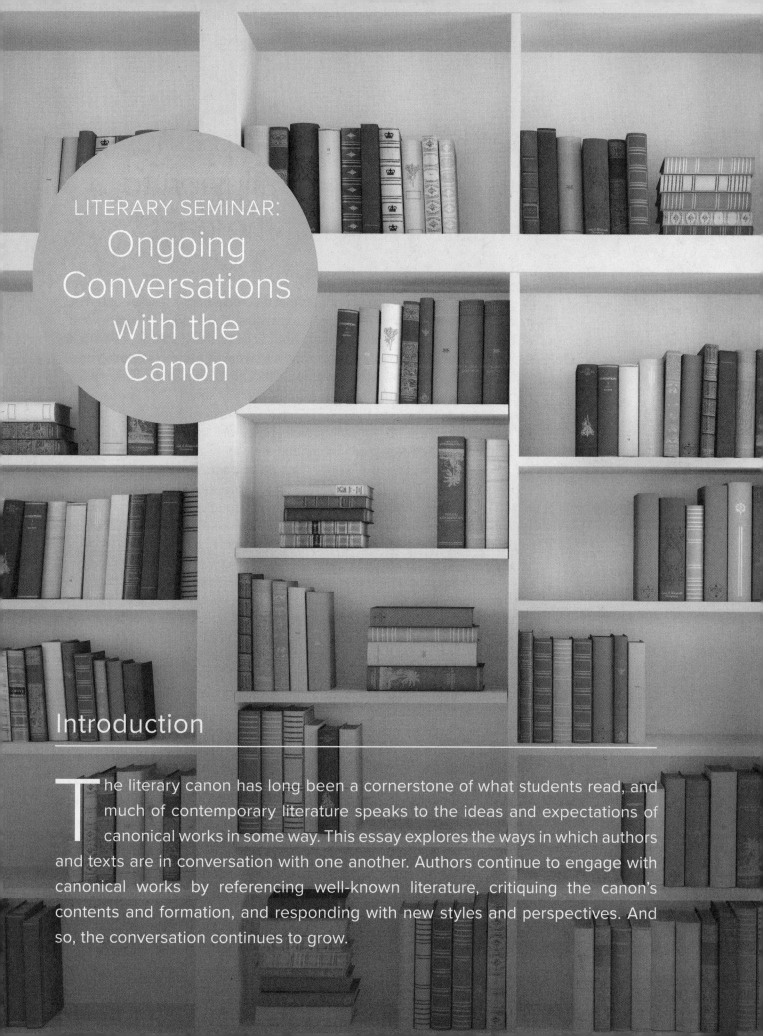

LITERARY SEMINAR:
Ongoing Conversations with the Canon

Introduction

The literary canon has long been a cornerstone of what students read, and much of contemporary literature speaks to the ideas and expectations of canonical works in some way. This essay explores the ways in which authors and texts are in conversation with one another. Authors continue to engage with canonical works by referencing well-known literature, critiquing the canon's contents and formation, and responding with new styles and perspectives. And so, the conversation continues to grow.

"It can be difficult to pick up a novel without some sort of allusion to significant works of the past."

NOTES

1   "It is a truth universally acknowledged that a zombie in possession of brains must be in want of more brains." So begins *Pride and Prejudice and Zombies*—a parallel novel that takes Austen's classic story of Regency-period family, marriage, and social dynamics and interweaves a zombie **apocalypse.** The updated classic has become a bestseller and follows a long line of work inspired by Jane Austen, including a time-travel TV series, *Lost in Austen;* a book about reading Jane Austen, *The Jane Austen Book Club;* and a Bollywood remake, *Bride and Prejudice.* These are but a few examples of ways that modern writers continue to interact with preexisting works, but to some extent, all writers can be thought of as participating in an ongoing conversation, explicitly or implicitly responding to the works and ideas of others. This interplay of ideas can be seen throughout literature through allusions, responses to previous ideas and themes, and even through choices to change the subject of the conversation altogether.

2   The English texts most consistently engaged with—those at the center of this conversation—have been those that are considered part of the Western literary canon. Originally, the word *canon* referred to a standard of judgment based on a list of authorized texts. Today, the canon typically refers to a list of works and authors generally considered essential reading for a Western literary education. When a work is said to be part of the canon, the speaker means to say it is a classic, considered an important work by scholars of literature. More specifically, the Western canon includes works dating from ancient Rome through the twentieth century and is composed of mostly English language writers who are deemed to carry "literary weight," from William Shakespeare to Willa Cather. Many educational institutions pull from the canon to construct literature curricula, to inform literary techniques and analysis, and to explain the development of literature over time. Schools teach these texts because they have been widely read over time and they provide a basis with which to compare other works. What's more, there is already a wealth of scholarship and teaching materials built around these texts, which further recommend them to instructors.

American author Willa Cather (1873–1947) as photographed in 1926. Cather was awarded the Pulitzer Prize for her novel *One of Ours* (1922).

Engaging with the Canon

3   As a set of texts that many people may already know, classics can often provide common ground between writers and readers to start a conversation between two texts. Consider the effectiveness of *Pride and Prejudice and Zombies*'s introduction. While it's funny enough on its own, it takes on new depth when a reader experiences a flash of recognition and surprise at the subversion of Austen's famous first line: "It is a truth universally acknowledged that a single man in possession of a fortune must be in want of a wife." In fact, it can be difficult to pick up a novel without some sort of allusion to significant works of the past. Some of the most influential writers in English, William Shakespeare and John Milton, made heavy use of allusions to biblical stories and events, and few authors have been as heavily quoted and referenced as Shakespeare.

4   Part of the power of allusions is the way that they serve as a shorthand to communicate a much larger and more nuanced meaning. It's a bit like a footnote that provides the reader access to a wealth of information and associations—so long as the reader catches the reference, of course, which is one reason there are so many allusions to canonical works. Take, for example, *Things Fall Apart* by Nigerian author Chinua Achebe, whose title makes reference to William Yeats's poem "The Second Coming" (its title is, itself, a Christian biblical allusion). The original poem tells the story of a time of deep upset and instability. The reference adds an air of foreboding before the first page has even been read. A reader familiar with Yeats's poem might encounter *Things Fall Apart* and fill in the next line of the poem themselves,

NOTES

"the center cannot hold," immediately illuminating many of the events and themes that will emerge in Achebe's novel. While the title works on a literal level for readers unfamiliar with the reference, the allusion takes the reader further by introducing the unsettling chaos already established by Yeats.

5 Authors can also use allusion to tap into a broader notion of what a work signifies. Chimamanda Adichie, a **contemporary** Nigerian author, published her story "Ghosts" in a collection titled *The Thing Around Your Neck*. The title alludes to Samuel Taylor Coleridge's poem "The Rime of the Ancient Mariner" and the albatross that hangs around the mariner's neck. The connection conveys a sense of burden, which Adichie relates to the immigrant experience. Through reference to the classic text, a core part of the traditional British curriculum imported through colonization, Adichie highlights a larger conversation—one that positions her work simultaneously inside and against the traditional canon. It both signals that Adichie is "in the know" and alerts the reader to a colonial presence, alongside any contemporary associations that may also echo through Adichie's choice of language.

Chimamanda Adichie speaking at the 2018 Action Against Hunger Gala in New York City

Building on What Came Before

6 Parallel novels, which go well beyond the status of allusion, provide a way for writers to build directly on previous texts. These works of fiction take place in, or are based on, the world created in a preexisting work, usually a "classic." A parallel novel may add a startling new element to a previous text, or it may catapult minor characters to the center of the story's narration, as Tom Stoppard's 1966 play *Rosencrantz and Guildenstern Are Dead* did for *Hamlet's* minor players. Because parallel novels often seek to tell stories from a new perspective, they can highlight voices that have traditionally been absent from the canon—either through the author's voice or through the

NOTES

voice of a character who was **marginalized** in the original work. In so doing, parallel novels can become an avenue to interrogate and reinvigorate the traditional canon. By making calculated choices about what part of a classic work to change and why, writers of parallel novels encourage readers to ask questions: How are those traditional stories told? How are those classics a reflection of their time? How do contemporary authors see the same story in a different way? How do those classic stories change when told from the perspective of another, less often heard, voice?

7   A classic of the parallel novel genre, *Wide Sargasso Sea* by Jean Rhys reveals the untold backstory of the "madwoman" from the classic novel *Jane Eyre* by Charlotte Brontë. Rhys, a Dominican author, opens her novel in Jamaica and tells the story of Mr. Rochester's first wife through a narrative focused on her experiences before her fateful role in Jane's Yorkshire-based tale. In *Jane Eyre,* Bertha is voiceless and described as mad; very little reason is given for her behavior. *Wide Sargasso Sea* reimagines this character as Antoinette (later to change her name to Bertha at Mr. Rochester's request)—a protagonist with agency. Her behavior and circumstances are given historical context as Rhys grapples with the power imbalances between Antoinette and her new English husband, based on gender, social status, and the legacy of colonialism. While *Wide Sargasso Sea* stands alone as its own story, it also prompts readers to reevaluate *Jane Eyre* through this different lens. If readers think about the events from Bertha's perspective instead of Jane's, how does the story change? What new patterns arise? The power of a parallel novel, then, is not only in the story it tells, but also in its ability to respond to a story readers already know and reshape the way readers think about it.

Jamaica, where Jean Rhys's *Wide Sargasso* Sea opens, presents a drastically different setting from the moors of Charlotte Brontë's *Jane Eyre*, on which Rhys's novel is based.

An Ongoing Conversation

8   While allusions and parallel novels are direct references to previous works, most of the "conversation" between texts plays out in more subtle ways. The dance of ideas over time creates a push and pull, as authors build on, or reject, the ideas, perspectives, and styles that have come before. This can be seen over the course of historical periods, as with the Enlightenment's ideals of logic and empiricism building on the humanistic focus of the Renaissance, and the Romantic's rebuttal to the apparent "coldness" of the Enlightenment. More contemporarily, Modernist and colonialist themes have been answered by postmodern and postcolonial ones, as works have engaged with the legacy of colonialism. The discourse is not limited to literature; political speeches, for instance, participate in the conversation.

9   What's more, the concept of a canon is by no means static. In the 1980s and '90s, a heated academic debate about the canon came to be dubbed "the canon wars." Critics called out the very concept of a canon for being limited and exclusionary. They pointed out that what is considered canonical is largely determined by people in positions of authority, such as tenured professors and department chairs at universities, and, therefore, reflects limited perspectives about what is great literature and what should be read. Critics of the canon continue to argue that exceptional literature has long been left out, as Virginia Woolf argued in her essay *A Room of One's Own* when she explored the hypothetical fate of Shakespeare's talented sister. Her work, Woolf suggested, would no doubt have been lost to **obscurity,** if she even had the chance to write it at all. Due in part to such **advocacy,** many agree that a wider range of exemplary works should be recognized in the canon and taught in school curriculums; however, debates continue about what exactly should be included in the canon or whether the canon is even a useful construct.

10 As writers continue to add their voices, the conversation grows to include more debates, more insights, more creativity. Whenever we read, we listen to the ideas of others that have come before, and when we write, we participate in that conversation, adding our own ideas to the public sphere where others may be influenced by them or choose to respond to them. We add new stories, we respond to old ones, and the body of "classic" works continues to expand. Today's best-selling new novel may very well become a canonical text taught in high school classrooms across the country in twenty years. As readers and writers, we all engage in this conversation, shaping the stories we want to be told. Who do you think the next generation of students should be reading?

Literary Seminar: Ongoing Conversations with the Canon

Read "Literary Seminar: Ongoing Conversations with the Canon." After you read, complete the Think Questions below.

 THINK QUESTIONS

1. What is controversial about the concept of a canon? Cite relevant evidence from the text in your response.

2. Why are parallel novels typically based on classic works of literature? Cite relevant evidence from the text in your response.

3. How might the reading experience of *Things Fall Apart* differ for a reader who is familiar with the references Achebe is making as compared to a reader unfamiliar with the references? Cite relevant evidence from the text in your response.

4. Use context clues to determine the meaning of the word ***marginalized*** as it is used in the text. Write your definition of *marginalized* here, along with words from the text you used to determine its meaning. Then check a dictionary to confirm your understanding.

5. What is the meaning of the word ***advocacy*** as it is used in the text? Write your best definition here, along with a brief explanation of how you arrived at its meaning.

Ghosts

FICTION
Chimamanda Ngozi Adichie
2009

Introduction

By the time Beyoncé famously sampled one of Nigerian writer Chimamanda Ngozi Adichie's speeches in the song "Flawless," Adichie's body of work— including her novels, essays, and short stories—had already earned her a MacArthur fellowship and a spot in the *New Yorker's* "20 Under 40" series. The daughter of Nigerian academics, Adichie (b. 1977) grew up in the same house where renowned author Chinua Achebe used to live. The story presented here, "Ghosts," weaves factual characters and events from Adichie's own history into the fictional story of a university professor, James Nwoye (Adichie's father's name), who encounters an old colleague he presumed had died in the Nigerian Civil War—37 years earlier.

"You're alive?" I asked.
I was quite shaken.

1 Today I saw Ikenna Okoro, a man I had long thought was dead. Perhaps I should have bent down, grabbed a handful of sand, and thrown it at him, in the way my people do to make sure a person is not a ghost. But I am an educated man, a retired professor of seventy-one, and I am supposed to have armed myself with enough science

Nigerian author Chimamanda Ngozi Adichie

to laugh indulgently at the ways of my people. I did not throw sand at him. I could not have done so even if I had wished to, anyway, since we met on the concrete grounds of the university bursary.[1]

2 I was there to ask about my pension, yet again. "Good day, Prof," the dried-looking clerk, Ugwuoke, said. "Sorry, the money has not come in."

3 The other clerk, whose name I have now forgotten, nodded and apologized as well, while chewing on a pink lobe of kolanut. They were used to this. I was used to this. So were the tattered men who were clustered under the mango tree, talking loudly. The education minister has stolen the pension money, one fellow said. Another said that it was the vice chancellor, who deposited the money in personal high-interest accounts. When I walked up to them, they greeted me and shook their heads apologetically about the situation as if my professor-level pension is somehow more important than their messenger-level or driver-level pensions. They called me Prof, as most people do, as the hawkers sitting next to their trays under the tree did. "Prof! Prof! Come and buy good banana!"

4 I chatted with Vincent, who was our driver when I was faculty dean in the eighties. "No pension for three years, Prof. This is why people retire and die," he said.

NOTES

Skill:
Textual Evidence

James explicitly resists the impulse to make sure Ikenna "is not a ghost." This supports the inference that James's education separates him from "the ways of [his] people." Will the story reveal whether Ikenna is a ghost?

---

1. **bursary** an institution's treasury

NOTES

5   "*O joka*," I said, although he, of course, did not need me to tell him how terrible it was.

6   "How is Nkiru, Prof? I trust she is well in America?" He always asks about our daughter. He often drove my wife, Ebere, and me to visit her at the College of Medicine in Enugu. I remember that when Ebere died, he came with his relatives for *mgbalu*² and gave a touching, if rather long, speech about how well Ebere treated him when he was our driver, how she gave him our daughter's old clothes for his children.

7   "Nkiru is well," I said.

8   "Please greet her for me when she calls, Prof."

9   "I will."

10   He talked for a while longer, about ours being a country that has not learned to say thank you, about the students in the hostels not paying him on time for mending their shoes, but it was his Adam's apple that held my attention; it bobbed alarmingly as if just about to pierce the wrinkled skin of his neck and pop out. Vincent must be in his early sixties—since the non-academic staff retire at sixty rather than sixty-five—but he looks older. He has little hair left. I quite remember his **incessant** chatter while he drove me to work in those days; I remember, too, that he was fond of reading my newspapers, a practice I did not encourage.

11   "Prof, won't you buy us banana? Hunger is killing us," one of the men said. He had a familiar face. I think he was Professor Eboh's gardener, next door. His tone had that half-teasing, half-serious quality, but I bought groundnuts and a bunch of bananas for them, although what they really needed was some moisturizer. Their faces and arms looked like ash. It is almost March but the Harmattan³ is still very much here: the dry winds, the crackling static on my clothes, the gritty dust on my eyelashes. I used more lotion than usual today, and Vaseline on my lips, but still the dryness made my palms and face feel tight. Ebere used to tease me about not moisturizing properly, especially in the Harmattan and sometimes would stop me and slowly rub her Nivea on my arms, my legs, my back. We have to take care of this lovely skin, she would say with that playful laughter of hers. She always said my complexion was the persuading trait, since I did not have any money like her other suitors. Seamless, she called it. I saw nothing particularly distinct in my dark umber tone, but I did come to preen a little with the passing years, with Ebere's massaging hands.

---

2. **mgbalu** a traditional Igbo burial ceremony
3. **the Harmattan** dry wind from the Sahara blowing into West Africa; also the name of the season when it comes, typically from November to March

12   "Thank you, Prof!" the men said, and then began to mock one another about who would do the dividing.

13   I stood around and listened to their talk. I was aware that they spoke more respectably because I was there: carpentry was not going well, children were ill, more money-lender troubles. They laughed often. Of course they nurse resentment, as they well should, but it has somehow managed to leave their spirits whole. I often wonder whether I would be like them if I did not have money saved from my appointments in the Federal Office of Statistics and if Nkiru did not insist on sending me dollars that I do not need. I doubt it; I would probably have hunched up like a tortoise shell and let my dignity whittle away.

14   Finally I said good-bye to them and walked toward my car, parked near the whistling pine trees that shield the Faculty of Education from the bursary. That was when I saw Ikenna Okoro.

15   He called out to me first. "James? James Nwoye, is it you?" He stood with his mouth open and I could see that his teeth are still complete. I lost one last year. I have refused to have what Nkiru calls "work" done, but I still felt rather sour at Ikenna's full set.

16   "Ikenna? Ikenna Okoro?" I asked in the tentative way one suggests something that cannot be: the coming to life of a man who died thirty-seven years ago.

17   "Yes, yes." Ikenna came closer, uncertainly. We shook hands, and then hugged briefly.

18   We were not good friends, Ikenna and I; I knew him fairly well in those days only because everyone knew him fairly well. It was he who climbed the podium at the Staff Club, he who would speak until he was hoarse and sweating, he who handed out simplified tenets of Nyerere, the type smudgy on cheap paper. The social sciences people had too much time on their hands and worshiped radicals of all sorts who were thought by those of us in the sciences to be empty vessels. We saw Ikenna differently. I'm not sure why, but we forgave his peremptory style and did not discard his pamphlets and rather admired the erudite asperity with which he blazed through issues. He is still a shrunken man with froglike eyes and light skin that has become discolored with age. One heard of him in those days and then struggled to hide great disappointment upon seeing him, because the depth of his rhetoric somehow demanded good looks. But then my people say that a famous animal does not always fill the hunter's basket.

19   "You're alive?" I asked. I was quite shaken. My family and I saw him on the day he died, 6 July, 1967, the day we evacuated in a hurry, with the sun a strange fiery red in the sky and nearby the *boom-boom-boom* of shelling as the federal soldiers advanced. We were in my Peugeot 404. The militia waved us through the campus gates and shouted that we should not worry, that the

Skill:
Story Elements

James listens to the men, noticing his effect on them. Their lives are difficult, but James admires their positive attitudes: they laugh a lot and have "whole" spirits.

Skill:
Story Elements

James is shocked to see Ikenna Okoro because he thought Ikenna had died. The author uses a flashback to give details about James and his family evacuating at the beginning of the war.

Please note that excerpts and passages in the StudySync® library and this workbook are intended as touchstones to generate interest in an author's work. The excerpts and passages do not substitute for the reading of entire texts, and StudySync® strongly recommends that students seek out and purchase the whole literary or informational work In order to experience it as the author intended. Links to online resellers are available in our digital library. In addition, complete works may be ordered through an authorized reseller by filling out and returning to StudySync® the order form enclosed in this workbook.

Reading & Writing Companion   43

vandals—as we called the federal soldiers—would be defeated in a matter of days and we could come back. The local villagers, the same ones who would pick through lecturers' dustbins for food after the war, were walking along, hundreds of them, women with boxes on their heads and babies tied to their backs, barefoot children carrying bundles, men dragging bicycles, holding yams. I remember that Ebere was consoling our daughter, Zik, about the doll left behind in our haste, when we saw Ikenna's green Kadet. He was driving the opposite way, back into campus. I horned and stopped. "You can't go back!" I called. But he waved and said, "I have to get some manuscripts." Or maybe he said, "I have to get some materials." I thought it rather foolhardy of him to go back in since the shelling sounded close and our troops would drive the vandals back in a week or two anyway. But I was also full of a sense of our collective invincibility, of the justness of the Biafran cause,[4] and so I did not think much else of it until we heard Nsukka fell on the very day we evacuated and the campus was occupied. The bearer of the news, a relative of Professor Ezike, also told us that two lecturers had been killed. One of them had argued with the federal soldiers before he was shot. We did not need to be told this was Ikenna.

20 Ikenna laughed. "I am, I am!" He seemed to find his own response even funnier because he laughed again. Even his laughter, now that I think of it, seemed discolored, hollow, nothing like the aggressive sound that reverberated all over the Staff Club in those days.

21 "But we saw you," I said. "You remember? That day we evacuated?"

22 "Yes," he said.

23 "They said you did not come out."

24 "I did." He nodded. "I did. I left Biafra the following month."

25 "You left?" It is incredible that I felt, today, a brief flash of that deep disgust that came when we heard of saboteurs—we called them sabos—who betrayed our soldiers, our just cause, our nascent nation, in exchange for a safe passage across to Nigeria, to the salt and meat and cold water that the blockade kept from us.

26 "No, no, it was not like that, not what you think." Ikenna paused and I noticed that his gray shirt sagged at the shoulders. "I went abroad on a Red Cross plane. I went to Sweden." There was an uncertainty about him, a **diffidence** that seemed alien, very unlike the man who so easily got people to *act*. I remember how he organized the rallies after Biafra was declared, all of us

4. **the Biafran cause** referring to the political struggle of the breakaway Republic of Biafra, an area of eastern Nigeria that fought in the Nigerian Civil War for independence from 1967 until defeat in 1970

crowded at Freedom Square while Ikenna talked and we cheered and shouted, "Happy Independence!"

27 "You went to Sweden?" I asked.

28 "Yes."

29 He said nothing else and I realized that he would not tell me more, that he would not tell me just how he had come out of the campus alive or how he came to be on that plane; I know of the children airlifted to Gabon later in the war but certainly not of people flown out on Red Cross planes, and so early, too. The silence between us was tense.

30 "Have you been in Sweden since?" I asked.

31 "Yes. My whole family was in Abagana when they bombed it. Nobody left, so there was no reason for me to come back." He stopped to let out a harsh sound that was supposed to be laughter but sounded more like a series of coughs. "I was in touch with Doctor Anya for a while. He told me about rebuilding our campus, and I think he said you left for America after the war."

32 In fact, Ebere and I came back to Nsukka right after the war ended in 1970, but only for a few days. It was too much for us. Our books were in a charred pile in the front garden, under the umbrella tree. The lumps of calcified feces in the bathtub were strewn with pages of my *Mathematical Annals*, used as toilet paper, crusted smears blurring the formulas I had studied and taught. Our piano—Ebere's piano—was gone. My graduation gown, which I had worn to receive my first degree at Ibadan, had been used to wipe something and now lay with ants crawling in and out, busy and oblivious to me watching them. Our photographs were ripped, their frames broken. So we left for America and did not come back until 1976. We were assigned a different house on Ezenweze Avenue and for a long time we avoided driving along Imoke Street, because we did not want to see the old house; we later heard that the new people had cut down the umbrella tree. I told Ikenna all of this, although I said nothing about our time at Berkeley, where my friend Chuck Bell arranged my teaching appointment. Ikenna was silent for a while, and then he said, "How is your little girl, Zik? She must be a grown woman now."

33 He always insisted on paying for Zik's Fanta when we took her to the Staff Club on Family Day because, he said, she was the prettiest of the children. I suspect it was really because we had named her after our president, and Ikenna was an early Zikist before claiming the movement was too tame and leaving.

34 "The war took Zik," I said in Igbo. Speaking of death in English has always had for me a disquieting finality.

NOTES

35 Ikenna breathed deeply, but all he said was "*Ndo*," nothing more than sorry. I am relieved he did not ask how—there are not many hows anyway—and that he did not look inordinately shocked, as if war deaths are ever really accidents.

36 "We had another child after the war, another daughter," I said. But Ikenna was talking in a rush. "I did what I could," he said. "I did. I left the International Red Cross. It was full of cowards who could not stand up for human beings. They backed down after that plane was shot down at Eket as if they did not know it was exactly what Gowon wanted. But the World Council of Churches kept flying in relief through Uli. At nights! I was there in Uppsala when they met. It was the biggest operation they had done since the Second World War. I organized the fundraising. I organized the Biafran rallies all over the European capitals. You heard about the big one at Trafalgar Square?[5] I was at the top of that. I did what I could."

37 I was not sure that Ikenna was speaking to me. It seemed that he was saying what he had said over and over to many people. I looked toward the mango tree. The men were still clustered there, but I could not tell whether they had finished the bananas and groundnuts. Perhaps it was then that I began to feel submerged in hazy nostalgia, a feeling that has still not left me.

38 "Chris Okigbo died, not so?" Ikenna asked and made me focus once again. For a moment, I wondered if he wanted me to deny that, to make Okigbo a ghost-come-back, too. But Okigbo died, our genius, our star, the man whose poetry moved us all, even those of us in the sciences.

39 "Yes, the war took Okigbo."

40 "We lost a colossus in the making."

41 "True, but at least he was brave enough to fight." As soon as I said that, I was regretful. I had meant it only as a tribute to Chris Okigbo, who could have worked at one of the directorates like the rest of us university people but instead took up a gun to defend Nsukka. I did not want Ikenna to misunderstand my intention and wondered whether to apologize. He looked away. A small dust whirl was building up across the road. The wind whipped dry leaves off the trees. Perhaps because of my discomfort, I began to tell Ikenna about the day we drove back to Nsukka, about the landscape of ruins, the blown-out roofs, the houses riddled with holes that Ebere said were rather like Swiss cheese. When we got to the road that runs through Aguleri, Biafran soldiers stopped us and shoved a wounded soldier into our car; his blood dripped onto the backseat and, because the upholstery had a tear, soaked deep into the stuffing, mingled with the very insides of our car. A stranger's blood. I was not sure why I chose this particular story to tell Ikenna, but to make it seem

---

5. **Trafalgar Square** public square in the city of Westminster, London, that is a site of major political demonstrations

worth his while I added that the metallic smell of the soldier's blood reminded me of him, Ikenna, because I had always imagined that the federal soldiers shot him and left him to die, left his blood to stain the street. This is not true; I neither imagined such a thing, nor did that wounded soldier remind me of Ikenna. If he thought my story strange, he did not say so. He nodded and said, "I've heard so many stories, so many."

42 "How is life in Sweden?" I asked.

43 He shrugged. "I retired last year. I decided to come back and see." He said "see" as if it meant something more than what one did with one's eyes.

44 "What about your family?" I asked.

45 "I never married."

46 "Oh," I said.

47 "And how is your wife doing? Nnenna, isn't it?" Ikenna asked.

48 "Ebere."

49 "Oh, yes, of course, Ebere. Lovely woman."

50 "Ebere fell asleep three years ago," I said in Igbo. I was surprised to see the tears that glassed Ikenna's eyes. He had forgotten her name and yet, somehow, he was capable of mourning her, or of mourning a time immersed in possibilities. I realize, now, that Ikenna is a man who carries with him the weight of what could have been.

51 "I'm so sorry," he said. "So sorry."

52 "It's all right," I said. "She visits."

53 "What?" he asked me with a perplexed look, although he, of course, had heard me.

54 "She visits. She visits me."

55 "I see," Ikenna said with that pacifying tone one reserves for the mad.

56 "I mean, she visited America quite often; our daughter is a doctor there."

57 "Oh, is that right?" Ikenna asked too brightly. He looked relieved. I don't blame him. We are the educated ones, taught to keep tightly rigid our boundaries of what is considered real. I was like him until Ebere first visited, three weeks after her funeral. Nkiru and her son had just returned to America. I was alone. When I heard the door downstairs close and open and close again, I thought nothing of it. The evening winds always did that. But there was no rustle of leaves outside my bedroom window, no *swish-swish* of the avocado and

Skill:
Textual Evidence

James says his wife "visits" him. When Ikenna appears "perplexed" and uses a "pacifying tone," James changes the subject. This supports the inference that James is worried about what others think about him seeing his wife's ghost.

cashew trees. There was *no* wind outside. Yet, the door downstairs was opening and closing. In retrospect, I doubt that I was as scared as I should have been. I heard the feet on the stairs, in much the same pattern as Ebere walked, heavier on each third step. I lay still in the darkness of our room. Then I felt my bedcover pulled back, the gently massaging hands on my arms and legs and chest, and a pleasant drowsiness overcame me—a drowsiness that I am still unable to fight off. I woke up, as I still do after her visits, with my skin supple and thick with the scent of Nivea.

58 I often want to tell Nkiru that her mother visits weekly in the Harmattan and less often during the rainy season, but she will finally have reason to come here and bundle me back with her to America and I will be forced to live a life cushioned by so much convenience that it is sterile. A life littered with what we call "opportunities." A life that is not for me. I wonder what would have happened if we had won the war. Perhaps we would not be looking overseas for those opportunities, and I would not need to worry about our grandson who does not speak Igbo, who, the last time he visited, did not understand why he was expected to say "good afternoon" to strangers, because in his world one has to justify simple courtesies. But who can tell? Perhaps nothing would have changed even if we had won.

59 "How does your daughter like America?" Ikenna asked.

60 "She is doing very well,"

61 "And you said she is a doctor?"

62 "Yes." I felt that Ikenna deserved to be told more, or maybe that the tension had not quite **abated,** so I said, "She lives in a small town in Connecticut, near Rhode Island. The hospital board had advertised for a doctor, and when she came they took one look at her and said they did not want a foreigner. But she is American-born—you see, we had her while at Berkeley—and so they were forced to let her stay." I chuckled, and hoped Ikenna would laugh along, too. But he did not.

63 "Ah, yes. At least it's not as bad now as it was for us. Remember what it was like schooling in *oyibo*-land[6] in the late fifties?" he asked.

64 I nodded to show I remembered, although Ikenna and I could not have had the same experience as students overseas; he is an Oxford man while I did not school in England at all.

65 "The Staff Club is a shell of what it used to be," Ikenna said. "I went there this morning."

---

6. *oyibo*-**land** a country of Western or white people

66 "I haven't been there in so long. Even before I retired, it got to the point where I felt too old and out of place there. These greenhorns[7] are inept. Nobody is teaching. Nobody has fresh ideas. It is university politics, politics, politics, while students buy grades with money or their bodies."

67 "Is that right?"

68 "Oh, yes. Things have fallen. Senate meetings have become personality cult battles. It's terrible. Remember Josephat Udeana?"

69 "The great dancer."

70 I was taken aback for a moment because it had been so long since I thought of Josephat as he was in those days, by far the best ballroom dancer we had on campus. "Yes, yes, he was," I said, and I felt a strange gratitude that Ikenna's memories were frozen at a time when I still thought Josephat to be a man of integrity. "Josephat was vice chancellor for six years and ran this place like his father's chicken coop. Money disappeared and then we would see new cars stamped with the names of foreign foundations that did not exist. Some people went to court, but nothing came of that. He dictated who would be promoted and who would be stagnated. In short, the man acted like a solo University Council. This present vice chancellor is following him faithfully. I have not been paid my pension since I retired, you know."

71 "And why isn't anybody doing something about all this? Why?" Ikenna asked, and for the briefest moment the old Ikenna was there, in the voice, the outrage, and I was reminded again that this was an intrepid man. Perhaps he would pound his fist on a nearby tree.

72 "Well," I shrugged. "Many of the lecturers are changing their official dates of birth. They go to Personnel Services and bribe somebody and add five years. Nobody wants to retire."

73 "It is not right. Not right at all."

74 "It's all over the country, really, not just here." I shook my head in that slow, side-to-side way that my people have perfected when referring to things of this sort, as if to say that the situation is, sadly, **ineluctable.**

75 "I was reading about fake drugs in the papers; it looks serious," Ikenna said, and I immediately thought it too convenient of a coincidence, his bringing up fake drugs. Selling expired medicine is the latest plague of our country, and if Ebere had not died the way she did, I would have found this to be a normal segue in the conversation. But I was suspicious. I wondered if Ikenna had heard how Ebere died and wanted to get me to talk about it, to exhibit a little more of the lunacy that he had already glimpsed.

---

7. **greenhorn** a newcomer or inexperienced person

NOTES

76 "Fake drugs are horrible," I said gravely, determined to say nothing else. But I may have been wrong about Ikenna's plot, because he did not pursue the subject. He asked me, "So what do you do these days?" He seemed curious, as if he were wondering just what kind of life I am leading here, alone, in a university town that is now a withered skin of what it used to be, waiting for a pension that never comes. I smiled and said that I am resting; is that not what one does on retiring?

77 Sometimes I drop by to visit my old friend Professor Maduewe. I take walks across the faded field of Freedom Square with the flame trees. Or along Ikejiani Avenue, where the motorcycles speed past, students perched astride, often coming too close to one another as they avoid the gaping potholes. In the rainy season, when I discover a new gully where the rains have eaten at the land, I feel a flush of accomplishment. I read newspapers. I eat well; my househelp, Harrison, comes five days a week and his onugbu soup is unparalleled. I talk to our daughter often, and when my phone goes dead every other week, I hurry to NITEL to bribe somebody to get it repaired. I unearth old, old journals in my dusty, cluttered study. I breathe in deeply the scent of the neem trees that screen my house from Professor Eboh's—a scent that is supposed to be medicinal, although I am no longer sure what it is said to cure. I do not go to church; I stopped going after Ebere first visited, because I was no longer uncertain. It is our diffidence about the afterdeath that leads us to religion. So on Sundays I sit on the veranda and watch the vultures stamp on my roof, and I imagine that they glance down in bemusement. "Is it a good life, Daddy?" Nkiru has taken to asking lately, with that faint, vaguely troubling American accent. It is not good or bad, I tell her, it is simply mine. And that is what matters.

78 I asked Ikenna to come back to my house with me, but he said he was on his way to Enugu, and when I asked if he would come by later, he made a vague motion with his hands that suggested assent. I know he will not come though. I will not see him again. I watched him walk away, this shriveled nut of a man, and I drove home thinking of the lives we might have had and the lives we did have, all of us who went to the Staff Club in those good days before the war.

79 Because of the minor scratch I had as I backed it out last week, I was careful parking my Mercedes in the garage. It is fifteen years old but runs quite well. I remember how excited Nkiru was when it was shipped back from Germany, where I bought it when I went to receive the Science Africana prize. It was the newest model. I did not know this, but her fellow teenagers did and they all came to look at it. Now, of course, everyone drives a Mercedes, imported secondhand from Cotonou. Ebere used to mock them, saying our car is old but much better than all those *tuke-tuke* things people are driving with no seatbelts. She still has that sense of humor. At her burial, when our grandson

read his poem, "Keep Laughing, Grandma," I thought the title perfect, and the childish words almost brought me to tears, despite my suspicion that Nkiru wrote most of them.

80   I looked around the yard as I walked indoors. Harrison does a little gardening, mostly watering in this season. The rose bushes are just dried stalks, but at least the hardy cherry bushes are a dusty green. I turned the TV on. It was still raining on the screen, although Doctor Otagbu's son, the bright young man who is reading electronics engineering, came last week to fix it. My satellite channels went off after the last thunderstorm. One can stay some weeks without BBC and CNN anyway, and the programs on NTA[8] are quite good when they are not showing half-naked, dancing American teenagers. It was NTA, some days ago, that broadcast an interview with yet another man accused of importing fake drugs—typhoid fever medicine in this case. "My drugs don't actually kill people," he said, helpfully, facing the camera as if in an appeal to the masses. "It is only that they will not cure your illness." I turned the TV off because I could no longer bear to see the man's blubbery lips. But I was not offended, not as egregiously as I would have been if Ebere did not visit. I only hoped that he would not be let free to go off once again to China or India or wherever they go to import expired medicine that will not actually kill people, but will only make sure the illness kills them.

81   I am sitting now in my study, where I helped Nkiru with her difficult secondary school math assignments. The armchair leather is solid and worn. The pastel paint above the bookshelves is peeling. I wonder why it never came up, throughout the years, that Ikenna did not die. True, we did sometimes hear stories of men who had been thought dead and who walked into their compounds months, even years, after January 1970; I can only imagine the quantity of sand poured on broken men by family members suspended between disbelief and hope. But we hardly talked about the war. When we did it was with an implacable vagueness, as if what mattered were not that we crouched in muddy bunkers during air raids after which we buried corpses with bits of pink on their charred skin, not that we ate cassava peels and watched our children's bellies swell, but that we survived. It was a **tacit** agreement among all of us, the survivors of Biafra. Even Ebere and I, who had debated our first child's name, Zik, for months, agreed very quickly on Nkiru: what is ahead is better. We will look forward, forward, forward.

"Ghosts" by Chimamanda Adichie. Copyright © 2009 by Chimamanda Ngozi Adichie, used by permission of The Wylie Agency LLC

---

8. **NTA** Nigerian Television Authority

GHOSTS

First Read

Read the short story "Ghosts." After you read, complete the Think Questions below.

1. Why did James Nwoye think Ikenna Okoro was dead? Cite evidence from the text.

2. What did James and his wife see when they visited their old home, and how did it affect them? Support your response with evidence from the text.

3. What is life in Nigeria like in the aftermath of the war? Cite specific examples from the text as support.

4. The narrator says about Ikenna Okoro, "There was an uncertainty about him, a **diffidence** that seemed alien, very unlike the man who so easily got people to *act*." Using context clues from this passage, explain what the word *diffidence* means.

5. The adjective *taciturn* is commonly used to describe someone who is quiet or withdrawn. With this in mind, what do you think a "**tacit** agreement" might be? Explain, in your own words, the meaning of this term in the final paragraph of the story.

Skill:
Textual Evidence

Use the Checklist to analyze Textual Evidence in "Ghosts." Refer to the sample student annotations about Textual Evidence in the text.

To support an analysis by citing evidence that is explicitly stated in the text, do the following:

✓ Read the text closely and critically.

✓ Identify what the text says explicitly.

✓ Find the most relevant textual evidence that supports your analysis.

✓ Consider why an author explicitly states specific details and information.

✓ Cite the specific words, phrases, sentences, or paragraphs from the text that support your analysis.

✓ Determine where evidence in the text still leaves certain matters uncertain or unresolved.

To interpret implicit meanings in a text by making inferences, do the following:

✓ Combine information directly stated in the text with your own knowledge, experiences, and observations.

✓ Cite the specific words, phrases, sentences, or paragraphs from the text that led to and support this inference.

To cite textual evidence, as well as inferences drawn from the text, to support an analysis of what the text says explicitly, consider the following questions:

✓ Have I read the text closely and critically?

✓ What inferences am I making about the text?

✓ What textual evidence am I using to support these inferences?

✓ Am I quoting the evidence from the text correctly?

✓ Does my textual evidence logically relate to my analysis or the inference I am making?

✓ Does evidence in the text still leave certain matters unanswered or unresolved? In what ways?

Skill:
Textual Evidence

Reread paragraph 58 of "Ghosts." Then use the Checklist on the previous page to answer the multiple-choice questions below.

♻ YOUR TURN

1. This question has two parts. First, answer Part A. Then, answer Part B.

    Part A: Which inference is best supported by this paragraph?

    ○ A. More opportunities exist in America than in Nigeria.

    ○ B. The narrator does not want to live in America.

    ○ C. The narrator loves Nigeria despite its problems.

    ○ D. Nkiru does not know about her mother's ghost.

    Part B: Which evidence from the paragraph best supports the answer to Part A?

    ○ A. "I often want to tell Nkiru that her mother visits weekly in the Harmattan and less often during the rainy season . . ."

    ○ B. ". . . I will be forced to live a life cushioned by so much convenience that it is sterile."

    ○ C. "I wonder what would have happened if we had won the war."

    ○ D. "Perhaps we would not be looking overseas for those opportunities . . ."

Skill:
Story Elements

Use the Checklist to analyze Story Elements in "Ghosts." Refer to the sample student annotations about Story Elements in the text.

••• CHECKLIST FOR STORY ELEMENTS

To identify the impact of the author's choices regarding how to develop and relate elements of a story or drama, note the following:

- ✓ where and when the story takes place, who the main characters are, and the main conflict, or problem, in the plot

- ✓ the order of the action

- ✓ how the author introduces and develops

- ✓ the impact the author's choice of setting has on the characters and their attempt to solve the problem

To analyze the impact of the author's choices regarding how to develop and relate elements of a story or drama, consider the following questions:

- ✓ How do the author's choices affect the story elements? The development of the plot?

- ✓ How does the setting influence the characters?

- ✓ Which elements of the setting affect the plot and, in particular, the problem the characters face and must solve?

- ✓ Do any flashbacks or other story elements have an effect on the development of events? How does the author's choice of using a flashback affect this development?

- ✓ How does the author introduce and develop characters in the story? Why do you think the author makes these choices?

Skill:
Story Elements

Reread paragraph 81 of "Ghosts." Then use the Checklist on the previous page to answer the multiple-choice questions below.

⟳ YOUR TURN

1. This question has two parts. First, answer Part A. Then, answer Part B.

   Part A: How do the setting details in this paragraph help the reader better understand the characters?

   ○ A. The details about the horrors of the war help the reader understand why the characters look toward the future instead of the past.

   ○ B. The details about James's study help the reader understand how much time has passed since James experienced the horrible war.

   ○ C. The details about dead men returning after the war help the reader understand that James is not the only character who sees ghosts.

   ○ D. The details about the horrors of the war help the reader understand what killed Zik and how Ikenna survived.

   Part B: Which evidence best supports the answer to Part A?

   ○ A. "I am sitting now in my study, where I helped Nkiru with her difficult secondary school math assignments."

   ○ B. "True, we did sometimes hear stories of men who had been thought dead and who walked into their compounds months, even years, after January 1970 . . ."

   ○ C. "When we did it was with an implacable vagueness, as if what mattered were not that we crouched in muddy bunkers during air raids after which we buried corpses with bits of pink on their charred skin . . ."

   ○ D. "Even Ebere and I, who had debated our first child's name, Zik, for months, agreed very quickly on Nkiru . . ."

2. Which statement best explains why the author ends the story with this paragraph?

   ○ A. The paragraph refers to the beginning of the story when James wants to throw sand at Ikenna.

   ○ B. The paragraph emphasizes the relationship between Ebere and James, which is the focus of the story.

   ○ C. The paragraph explains that Ikenna is not the only one to return after so many years.

   ○ D. The paragraph clarifies some of James's past and his outlook on the present.

Close Read

GHOSTS

Reread "Ghosts." As you reread, complete the Skills Focus questions below. Then use your answers and annotations from the questions to help you complete the Write activity.

◎ SKILLS FOCUS

1. Identify a detail that introduces the social and economic setting, and explain why this detail is effective in helping readers understand the theme of the story.

2. Identify James's reaction to his interaction with the men he buys groundnuts and bananas from. Infer and explain an implicit meaning evident in the textual evidence. Does anything still remain unresolved?

3. Highlight a passage in which James speaks in Igbo, and explain how the relationship between characterization and point of view in the passage helps develop a theme in the story.

4. Identify an example of vivid sensory language, and explain how it helps shape the reader's perception of characters and events in the story.

5. Reread paragraphs 42–51. In what ways has the change caused by war brought these two men closer together and helped them better understand each other? In what ways has the war separated them and increased their differences?

✎ WRITE

COMPARE AND CONTRAST: In many ways, "Ghosts" has two main characters: James Nwoye, the narrator, and Ikenna Okoru, James's former colleague. How are the personalities and experiences of these two men different? How are they similar? What do their stories, taken together, tell you about the Nigerian Civil War and its inevitable effects on Nigeria? Support your ideas with textual evidence.

Love After Love

POETRY
Derek Walcott
1976

Introduction

Derek Walcott (1930–2017), professor, playwright, and poet, won the Nobel Prize in Literature in 1992 in recognition of his poetry. In brief lyrical verse and epic poems, Walcott, who was born in Saint Lucia, wrote of the Caribbean experience with a perspective that shifted from one as intimate as its tiptoeing lizards to one as large-scale as the cultural scars of colonialism. "Love After Love" is one of the great 20th-century poet's most beloved works.

"You will love again the stranger who was your self."

NOTES

1 The time will come
2 when, with **elation**
3 you will greet yourself arriving
4 at your own door, in your own mirror
5 and each will smile at the other's welcome,

6 and say, sit here. Eat.
7 You will love again the stranger who was your self.
8 Give wine. Give bread. Give back your heart
9 to itself, to the stranger who has loved you

10 all your life, whom you ignored
11 for another, who knows you by heart.
12 Take down the love letters from the bookshelf,

13 the photographs, the **desperate** notes,
14 peel your own image from the mirror.
15 Sit. Feast on your life.

Derek Walcott in Saint Malo, France

"Love After Love" from THE POETRY OF DEREK WALCOTT 1948–2013 by Derek Walcott, selected by Glyn Maxwell

✏ WRITE

DISCUSSION: Derek Walcott's poem "Love After Love" is a free-verse poem written in a conversational style that gives advice to readers. Work in pairs and groups to analyze the form, sound, and graphics of the poem. Notice the graphical elements of enjambment and punctuation, as well as the repetition of words and phrases. Consider how these elements affect the sound of the poem. Have one volunteer read the poem aloud. Then work in pairs or as a group to change the graphical elements. For instance, you might take out the enjambment or rewrite the text to avoid a comma or period within a line. In other words, change the shape and look of the poem on the page. Then have another volunteer read aloud the revised poem. Finally, discuss the effects of a poet's choice of form and graphics on the sound of the poem and the expression of meaning.

The Museum

FICTION

Leila Aboulela

1999

Introduction

Much like Shadia, the main character in her award-winning story "The Museum," author Leila Aboulela (b. 1964) grew up in Khartoum, the capital of Sudan, before moving as a young woman to Aberdeen, Scotland. Experiencing firsthand the cultural divide between Islam and the West would serve as the inspiration for much of Aboulela's writing, which explores issues of identity, migration, and Islamic spirituality. "The Museum" is one of her earliest published stories, yet it displays all the hallmarks of her best work, which has been translated into 14 languages and even adapted into a series of plays by BBC Radio.

"We have 7UP in Africa, and some people, a few people, have bathrooms with golden taps . . ."

1   At first Shadia was afraid to ask him for his notes. The earring made her afraid; the straight long hair that he had tied up with a rubber band. She had never seen a man with an earring and such long hair. But then she had never known such cold, so much rain. His silver earring was the strangeness of the West, another culture shock. She stared

Sudanese writer Leila Aboulela

at it during classes, her eyes straying from the white scribbles on the board. Most times she could hardly understand anything. Only the notation was familiar. But how did it all fit together? How did *this* formula lead to *this*? Her ignorance and the impending exams were horrors she wanted to escape. His long hair was a dull colour between yellow and brown. It reminded her of a doll she had when she was young. She had spent hours combing that doll's hair, stroking it. She had longed for such straight hair. When she went to Paradise she would have hair like that. When she ran it would fly behind her; if she bent her head down it would fall over her like silk and sweep the flowers on the grass. She watched his ponytail move as he wrote and then looked up at the board. She pictured her doll, vivid suddenly, after years, and felt sick that she was daydreaming in class, not learning a thing.

2   The first days of term, when the classes started for the M.Sc. in Statistics, she was like someone tossed around by monstrous waves—battered, as she lost her way to the different lecture rooms, fumbled with the photocopying machine, could not find anything in the library. She could scarcely hear or eat or see. Her eyes bulged with fright, watered from the cold. The course required a certain background, a background she didn't have. So she **floundered,** she and the other African students, the two Turkish girls, and the men from Brunei. Asafa, the short, round-faced Ethiopian, said, in his grave voice—as this collection from the Third World whispered their anxieties in grim Scottish corridors, the girls in nervous giggles—'Last year, last year a Nigerian on this very same course committed suicide. *Cut his wrists.*'

3 Us and them, she thought. The ones who would do well, the ones who would crawl and sweat and barely pass. Two predetermined groups. Asafa, generous and wise (he was the oldest), leaned over and whispered to Shadia: 'The Spanish girl is good. Very good.' His eyes bulged redder than Shadia's. He cushioned his fears every night in the university pub; she only cried. Their countries were next-door neighbours but he had never been to Sudan, and Shadia had never been to Ethiopia. 'But we met in Aberdeen!' she had shrieked when this information was exchanged, giggling furiously. Collective fear had its **euphoria.**

4 'That boy Bryan,' said Asafa, 'is excellent.'

5 'The one with the earring?'

6 Asafa laughed and touched his own unadorned ear. 'The earring doesn't mean anything. He'll get the Distinction. He was an undergraduate here; got First Class Honours. That gives him an advantage. He knows all the lecturers, he knows the system.'

7 So the idea occurred to her of asking Bryan for the notes of his graduate year. If she strengthened her background in stochastic processes and time series, she would be better able to cope with the new material they were bombarded with every day. She watched him to judge if he was approachable. Next to the courteous Malaysian students, he was devoid of manners. He mumbled and slouched and did not speak with respect to the lecturers. He spoke to them as if they were his equals. And he did silly things. When he wanted to throw a piece of paper in the bin, he squashed it into a ball and aimed at the bin. If he missed, he muttered under his breath. She thought that he was immature. But he was the only one who was sailing through the course.

8 The glossy handbook for overseas students had explained about the 'famous British reserve' and hinted that they should be grateful, things were worse further south, less 'hospitable.' In the cafeteria, drinking coffee with Asafa and the others, the picture of 'hospitable Scotland' was something different. Badr, the Malaysian, blinked and whispered, 'Yesterday our windows got smashed; my wife today is afraid to go out.'

9 'Thieves?' asked Shadia, her eyes wider than anyone else's.

10 'Racists,' said the Turkish girl, her lipstick chic, the word tripping out like silver, like ice.

11 Wisdom from Asafa, muted, before the collective silence: 'These people think they own the world . . .' and around them the aura of the dead Nigerian student. They were ashamed of that brother they had never seen. He had weakened, caved in. In the cafeteria, Bryan never sat with them. They never

sat with him. He sat alone, sometimes reading the local paper. When Shadia walked in front of him he didn't smile. 'These people are strange . . . One day they greet you, the next day they don't . . .'

12   On Friday afternoon, as everyone was ready to leave the room after Linear Models, she gathered her courage and spoke to Bryan. He had spots on his chin and forehead, was taller than her, restless, as if he was in a hurry to go somewhere else. He put his calculator back in its case, his pen in his pocket. She asked him for his notes, and his blue eyes behind his glasses took on the blankest look she had ever seen in her life. What was all the surprise for? Did he think she was an insect? Was he surprised that she could speak?

13   A mumble for a reply, words strung together. So taken aback, he was. He pushed his chair back under the table with his foot.

14   'Pardon?'

15   He slowed down, separated each word. 'Ah'll have them for ye on Monday.'

16   'Thank you.' She spoke English better than he did! How pathetic. The whole of him was pathetic. He wore the same shirt every blessed day. Grey and white stripe.

. . .

17   On the weekends, Shadia never went out of the halls and, unless someone telephoned long-distance from home, she spoke to no one. There was time to remember Thursday nights in Khartoum: a wedding to go to with Fareed, driving in his red Mercedes. Or the club with her sisters. Sitting by the pool drinking lemonade with ice, the waiters all dressed in white. Sometimes people swam at night, dived in the water—dark like the sky above. Here, in this country's weekend of Saturday and Sunday, Shadia washed her clothes and her hair. Her hair depressed her. The damp weather made it frizz up after she straightened it with hot tongs. So she had given up and now wore it in a bun all the time, tightly pulled back away from her face, the curls held down by pins and Vaseline Tonic. She didn't like this style, her corrugated hair, and in the mirror her eyes looked too large. The mirror in the public bathroom, at the end of the corridor to her room, had printed on it: 'This is the face of someone with HIV.' She had written about this mirror to her sister, something foreign and sensational like hail, and cars driving on the left. But she hadn't written that the mirror made her feel as if she had left her looks behind in Khartoum.

18   On the weekends, she made a list of the money she had spent: the sterling enough to keep a family alive back home. Yet she might fail her exams after all that expense, go back home empty-handed without a degree. Guilt was cold like the fog of this city. It came from everywhere. One day she forgot to

Copyright © BookheadEd Learning, LLC

pray in the morning. She reached the bus stop and then realized she hadn't prayed. That morning folded out like the nightmare she sometimes had, of discovering that she had gone out into the street without any clothes.

19   In the evening, when she was staring at multidimensional scaling, the telephone in the hall rang. She ran to answer it. Fareed's cheerful greeting: 'Here, Shadia, Mama and the girls want to speak to you.' His mother's endearments: 'They say it's so cold where you are . . .'

20   Shadia was engaged to Fareed. Fareed was a package that came with the 7UP franchise, the paper factory, the big house he was building, his sisters and widowed mother. Shadia was going to marry them all. She was going to be happy and make her mother happy. Her mother deserved happiness after the misfortunes of her life. A husband who left her for another woman. Six girls to bring up. People felt sorry for her mother. Six girls to educate and marry off. But your Lord is generous: each of the girls, it was often said, was lovelier than the other. They were clever too: dentist, pharmacist, architect, and all with the best of manners.

21   'We are just back from looking at the house.' Fareed's turn again to talk. 'It's coming along fine, they're putting the tiles down . . .'

22   'That's good, that's good,' her voice strange from not talking to anyone all day.

23   'The bathroom suites. If I get them all the same colour for us and the girls and Mama, I could get them on a discount. Blue, the girls are in favour of blue,' his voice echoed from one continent to another. Miles and miles.

24   'Blue is nice. Yes, better get them all the same colour.'

25   He was building a block of flats, not a house. The ground-floor flat for his mother and the girls until they married, the first floor for him and Shadia. When Shadia had first got engaged to Fareed, he was the son of a rich man. A man with the franchise for 7UP and the paper factory which had a monopoly[1] in ladies' sanitary towels. Fareed's sisters never had to buy sanitary towels; their house was abundant with boxes of *Pinky,* fresh from the production line. But Fareed's father died of an unexpected heart attack soon after the engagement party (five hundred guests at the Hilton). Now Shadia was going to marry the rich man himself. 'You are a lucky, lucky girl,' her mother had said, and Shadia had rubbed soap in her eyes so that Fareed would think she was weeping about his father's death.

26   There was no time to talk about her course on the telephone, no space for her anxieties. Fareed was not interested in her studies. He had said, 'I am

1. **monopoly** complete and exclusive control over something

very broad-minded to allow you to study abroad. Other men would not have put up with this . . .' It was her mother who was keen for her to study, to get a postgraduate degree from Britain and then have a career after she got married. 'This way,' her mother had said, 'you will have your in-laws' respect. They have money but you have a degree. Don't end up like me. I left my education to marry your father and now . . .' Many conversations ended with her mother bitter; with her mother saying, 'No one suffers like I suffer,' and making Shadia droop. At night her mother sobbed in her sleep, noises that woke Shadia and her sisters.

27   No, on the long-distance line, there was no space for her worries. Talk about the Scottish weather. Picture Fareed, generously perspiring, his stomach straining the buttons of his shirt. Often she had nagged him to lose weight, without success. His mother's food was too good; his sisters were both overweight. On the long-distance line, listen to the Khartoum gossip as if listening to a radio play.

28   On Monday, without saying anything, Bryan slid two folders across the table towards her as if he did not want to come near her, did not want to talk to her. She wanted to say, 'I won't take them till you hand them to me politely.' But smarting, she said, 'Thank you very much.' *She* had manners. *She* was well brought up.

29   Back in her room, at her desk, the clearest handwriting she had ever seen. Sparse on the pages, clean. Clear and rounded like a child's, the tidiest notes. She cried over them, wept for no reason. She cried until she wetted one of the pages, smudged the ink, blurred one of the formulas. She dabbed at it with a tissue but the paper flaked and became transparent. Should she apologize about the stain, say that she was drinking water, say that it was rain? Or should she just keep quiet, hope he wouldn't notice? She chided herself for all that concern. *He* wasn't concerned about wearing the same shirt every day. She was giving him too much attention thinking about him. He was just an immature and closed-in sort of character. He probably came from a small town, his parents were probably poor, low-class. In Khartoum, she never mixed with people like that. Her mother liked her to be friends with people who were higher up. How else were she and her sisters going to marry well? She must study the notes and stop crying over this boy's handwriting. His handwriting had nothing to do with her, nothing to do with her at all.

30   Understanding after not understanding is a fog lifting, pictures swinging into focus, missing pieces slotting into place. It is fragments gelling, a sound vivid whole, a basis to build on. His notes were the knowledge she needed, the gap filled. She struggled through them, not skimming them with the carelessness of incomprehension, but taking them in, making them a part of her, until in the depth of concentration, in the late hours of the nights, she lost awareness of time and place, and at last, when she slept she became epsilon

and gamma, and she became a variable, making her way through discrete space from state 'i' to state 'j.'

...

31   It felt natural to talk to him. As if now that she had spent hours and days with his handwriting, she knew him in some way. She forgot the offence she had taken when he had slid his folders across the table to her, all the times he didn't say hello.

32   In the computer room, at the end of the Statistical Packages class, she went to him and said: 'Thanks for the notes. They are really good. I think I might not fail, after all. I might have a chance to pass.' Her eyes were dry from all the nights she had stayed up. She was tired and grateful.

33   He nodded and they spoke a little about the Poisson distribution,[2] queuing theory.[3] Everything was clear in his mind; his brain was a clear pane of glass where all the concepts were written out boldly and neatly. Today, he seemed more at ease talking to her, though he still shifted about from foot to foot, avoiding her eyes.

34   He said, 'Do ye want to go for a coffee?'

35   She looked up at him. He was tall and she was not used to speaking to people with blue eyes. Then she made a mistake. Perhaps because she had been up late last night, she made that mistake. Perhaps there were other reasons for that mistake. The mistake of shifting from one level to another.

36   She said, 'I don't like your earring.'

37   The expression in his eyes, a focusing, no longer shifting away. He lifted his hand to his ear and tugged the earring off. His earlobe without the silver looked red and scarred.

38   She giggled because she was afraid, because he wasn't smiling, wasn't saying anything. She covered her mouth with her hand, then wiped her forehead and eyes. A mistake had been made and it was too late to go back. She plunged ahead, careless now, reckless. 'I don't like your long hair.'

39   He turned and walked away.

...

2. **Poisson distribution** a probability distribution formula developed by French mathematician Siméon Denis Poisson (1781–1840) to predict the frequency of events in a fixed interval
3. **queuing theory** involving the mathematical study of queues, or lines

40   The next morning, Multivariate Analysis, and she came in late, dishevelled from running and the rain. The professor, whose name she wasn't sure of (there were three who were Mc-something), smiled, unperturbed. All the lecturers were relaxed and **urbane,** in tweed jackets and polished shoes. Sometimes she wondered how the incoherent Bryan, if he did pursue an academic career, was going to transform himself into a professor like that. But it was none of her business.

41   Like most of the other students, she sat in the same seat in every class. Bryan sat a row ahead which was why she could always look at his hair. But he had cut it, there was no ponytail today! Just his neck and the collar of the grey and white striped shirt.

42   Notes to take down. *In discriminant analysis, a linear combination of variables serves as the basis for assigning cases to groups.*

43   She was made up of layers. Somewhere inside, deep inside, under the crust of vanity, in the untampered-with essence, she would glow and be in awe, and be humble and think, this is just for me, he cut his hair for me. But there were other layers, bolder, more to the surface. Giggling. Wanting to catch hold of a friend. Guess what? You wouldn't *believe* what this idiot did!

44   *Find a weighted average of variables . . . The weights are estimated so that they result in the best separation between the groups.*

45   After the class he came over and said very seriously, without a smile, 'Ah've cut my hair.'

46   A part of her hollered with laughter, sang: 'You stupid boy, you stupid boy, I can see that, can't I?'

47   She said, 'It looks nice.' She said the wrong thing and her face felt hot and she made herself look away so that she would not know his reaction. It was true though, he did look nice; he looked decent now.

. . .

48   She should have said to Bryan, when they first held their coffee mugs in their hands and were searching for an empty table, 'Let's sit with Asafa and the others.' Mistakes follow mistakes. Across the cafeteria, the Turkish girl saw them together and raised her perfect eyebrows. Badr met Shadia's eyes and quickly looked away. Shadia looked at Bryan and he was different, different without the earring and the ponytail, transformed in some way. If he would put lemon juice on his spots . . . but it was none of her business. Maybe the boys who smashed Badr's windows looked like Bryan, but with fiercer eyes, no glasses. She must push him away from her. She must make him dislike her.

49 He asked her where she came from and when she replied, he said, 'Where's that?'

50 'Africa,' with sarcasm. 'Do you know where *that* is?'

51 His nose and cheeks under the rims of his glasses went red. Good, she thought, good. He will leave me now in peace.

52 He said, 'Ah know Sudan is in Africa, I meant where exactly in Africa.'

53 'Northeast, south of Egypt. Where are *you* from?'

54 'Peterhead. It's north of here. By the sea.'

55 It was hard to believe that there was anything north of Aberdeen. It seemed to her that they were on the northernmost corner of the world. She knew better now than to imagine suntanning and sandy beaches for his 'by the sea.' More likely dismal skies, pale, bad-tempered people shivering on the rocky shore.

56 'Your father works in Peterhead?'

57 'Aye, he does.'

58 She had grown up listening to the proper English of the BBC World Service only to come to Britain and find people saying 'yes' like it was said back home in Arabic: 'aye.'

59 'What does he do, your father?'

60 He looked surprised, his blue eyes surprised. 'Ma dad's a joiner.'

61 Fareed hired people like that to work on the house. Ordered them about.

62 'And your mother?' she asked.

63 He paused a little, stirred sugar in his coffee with a plastic spoon. 'She's a lollipop lady.'

64 Shadia smirked into her coffee, took a sip.

65 'My father,' she said proudly, 'is a doctor, a specialist.' Her father was a gynaecologist. The woman who was now his wife had been one of his patients. Before that, Shadia's friends had teased her about her father's job, crude jokes that made her laugh. It was all so sordid now.

66 'And my mother,' she blew the truth up out of proportion, 'comes from a very big family. A ruling family. If you British hadn't colonized us, my mother would have been a princess now.'

67   'Ye walk like a princess,' he said.

68   What a gullible, silly boy! She wiped her forehead with her hand and said, 'You mean I am **conceited** and proud?'

69   'No, Ah didnae mean that, no . . .' The packet of sugar he was tearing open tipped from his hand, its contents scattered over the table. 'Ah . . . sorry . . .' He tried to scoop up the sugar and knocked against his coffee mug, spilling a little on the table.

70   She took out a tissue from her bag, reached over and mopped up the stain. It was easy to pick up all the bits of sugar with the damp tissue.

71   'Thanks,' he mumbled and they were silent. The cafeteria was busy: full of the humming, buzzing sound of people talking to each other, trays and dishes. In Khartoum, she avoided being alone with Fareed. She preferred it when they were with others: their families, their many natural friends. If they were ever alone, she imagined that her mother or her sister was with them, could hear them, and she spoke to Fareed with that audience in mind.

72   Bryan was speaking to her, saying something about rowing on the River Dee. He went rowing on the weekends, he belonged to a rowing club.

73   To make herself pleasing to people was a skill Shadia was trained in. It was not difficult to please people. Agree with them, never dominate the conversation, be economical with the truth. Now, here was someone to whom all these rules needn't apply.

74   She said to him, 'The Nile is superior to the Dee. I saw your Dee, it is nothing, it is like a stream. There are two Niles, the Blue and the White, named after their colours. They come from the south, from two different places. They travel for miles over countries with different names, never knowing they will meet. I think they get tired of running alone, it is such a long way to the sea. They want to reach the sea so that they can rest, stop running. There is a bridge in Khartoum, and under this bridge the two Niles meet. If you stand on the bridge and look down you can see the two waters mixing together.'

75   'Do ye get homesick?' he asked. She felt tired now, all this talk of the river running to rest in the sea. She had never talked like this before. Luxury words, and this question he asked.

76   'Things I should miss I don't miss. Instead I miss things I didn't think I would miss. The *azan*, the Muslim call to prayer from the mosque. I don't know if you know about it. I miss that. At dawn it used to wake me up. I would hear 'prayer is better than sleep' and just go back to sleep. I never got up to pray.' She looked down at her hands on the table. There was no relief in confessions, only his smile, young, and something like wonder in his eyes.

77 'We did Islam in school,' he said. 'Ah went on a trip to Mecca.'[4] He opened out his palms on the table.

78 'What!'

79 'In a book.'

80 'Oh.'

81 The coffee was finished. They should go now. She should go to the library before the next lecture and photocopy previous exam papers. Asafa, full of helpful advice, had shown her where to find them.

82 'What is your religion?' she asked.

83 'Dunno, nothing I suppose.'

84 'That's terrible! That's really terrible!' Her voice was too loud, concerned.

85 His face went red again and he tapped his spoon against the empty mug.

86 Waive all politeness, make him dislike her. Badr had said, even before his windows got smashed, that here in the West they hate Islam. Standing up to go, she said **flippantly,** 'Why don't you become a Muslim then?'

87 He shrugged. 'Ah wouldnae mind travelling to Mecca, I was keen on that book.'

88 Her eyes filled with tears. They blurred his face when he stood up. In the West they hate Islam and he . . . She said, 'Thanks for the coffee,' and walked away, but he followed her.

89 'Shadiya, Shadiya,' he pronounced her name wrongly, three syllables instead of two, 'there's this museum about Africa. I've never been before. If you'd care to go, tomorrow . . .'

90 No sleep for the guilty, no rest, she should have said no, I can't go, no I have too much catching up to do. No sleep for the guilty, the memories come from another continent. Her father's new wife, happier than her mother, fewer worries. When Shadia visits she offers fruit in a glass bowl, icy oranges and guavas, soothing in the heat. Shadia's father hadn't wanted a divorce, hadn't wanted to leave them; he wanted two wives, not a divorce. But her mother had too much pride, she came from fading money, a family with a 'name.'

91 Tomorrow she need not show up at the museum, even though she said that she would. She should have told Bryan she was engaged to be married,

---

4. **Mecca** the holiest city of the Islamic religion, located in Saudi Arabia, which Muslims face during the regular call to prayer

mentioned it casually. What did he expect from her? Europeans had different rules, reduced, abrupt customs. If Fareed knew about this . . . her secret thoughts like snakes . . . Perhaps she was like her father, a traitor. Her mother said that her father was devious. Sometimes Shadia was devious. With Fareed in the car, she would deliberately say, 'I need to stop at the grocer, we need things at home.' At the grocer he would pay for all her shopping and she would say, 'No, you shouldn't do that, no, you are too generous, you are embarrassing me.' With the money she saved, she would buy a blouse for her mother, nail varnish for her mother, a magazine, imported apples.

. . .

92   It was strange to leave her desk, lock her room and go out on a Saturday. In the hall the telephone rang. It was Fareed. If he knew where she was going now . . . Guilt was like a hard boiled egg stuck in her chest. A large cold egg.

93   'Shadia, I want you to buy some of the fixtures for the bathrooms. Taps and towel hangers. I'm going to send you a list of what I want exactly and the money . . .'

94   'I can't, I can't.'

95   'What do you mean you can't? If you go into any large department store . . .'

96   'I can't, I wouldn't know where to put these things, how to send them.'

97   There was a rustle on the line and she could hear someone whispering, Fareed distracted a little. He would be at work this time in the day, glass bottles filling up with clear effervescent, the words 7UP written in English and Arabic, white against the dark green.

98   'You can get good things, things that aren't available here. Gold would be good. It would match . . .'

99   Gold. Gold toilet seats!

100 'People are going to burn in hell for eating out of gold dishes, you want to sit on gold!'

101 He laughed. He was used to getting his own way, not easily threatened. 'Are you joking with me?'

102 'No.'

103 In a quieter voice, 'This call is costing . . .'

104 She knew, she knew. He shouldn't have let her go away. She was not coping with the whole thing, she was not handling the stress. Like the Nigerian student.

NOTES

105 'Shadia, gold-coloured, not gold. It's smart.'

106 'Allah is going to punish us for this, it's not right . . .'

107 'Since when have you become so religious!'

. . .

108 Bryan was waiting for her on the steps of the museum, familiar-looking against the strange grey of the city streets where cars had their headlamps on in the middle of the afternoon. He wore a different shirt, a navy-blue jacket. He said, not looking at her, 'Ah was beginning to think you wouldnae turn up.'

109 There was no entry fee to the museum, no attendant handing out tickets. Bryan and Shadia walked on soft carpets; thick blue carpets that made Shadia want to take off her shoes. The first thing they saw was a Scottish man from Victorian times. He sat on a chair surrounded by possessions from Africa: overflowing trunks, an ancient map strewn on the floor of the glass cabinet. All the light in the room came from this and other glass cabinets and gleamed on the waxed floors. Shadia turned away; there was an ugliness in the lifelike wispiness of his hair, his determined expression, the way he sat. A hero who had gone away and come back, laden, ready to report.

110 Bryan began to conscientiously study every display cabinet, to read the posters on the wall. She followed him around and thought that he was studious, careful; that was why he did so well in his degree. She watched the intent expression on his face as he looked at everything. For her the posters were an effort to read, the information difficult to take in. It had been so long since she had read anything outside the requirements of the course. But she persevered, saying the words to herself, moving her lips . . . *'During the 18th and 19th centuries, northeast Scotland made a disproportionate impact on the world at large by contributing so many skilled and committed individuals. In serving an empire they gave and received, changed others and were themselves changed and often returned home with tangible reminders of their experiences.'*

111 The tangible reminders were there to see, preserved in spite of the years. Her eyes skimmed over the disconnected objects out of place and time. Iron and copper, little statues. Nothing was of her, nothing belonged to her life at home, what she missed. Here was Europe's vision, the clichés about Africa: cold and odd.

112 She had not expected the dim light and the hushed silence. Apart from Shadia and Bryan, there was only a man with a briefcase, a lady who took down notes, unless there were others out of sight on the second floor. Something electrical, the heating of the lights, gave out a humming sound like that of an air conditioner. It made Shadia feel as if they were in an aeroplane without windows, detached from the world outside.

113 'He looks like you, don't you think?' she said to Bryan. They stood in front of a portrait of a soldier who died in the first year of the twentieth century. It was the colour of his eyes and his hair. But Bryan did not answer her, did not agree with her. He was preoccupied with reading the caption. When she looked at the portrait again, she saw that she was mistaken. That strength in the eyes, the purpose, was something Bryan didn't have. They had strong faith in those days long ago.

114 Biographies of explorers who were educated in Edinburgh; they knew what to take to Africa: doctors, courage, Christianity, commerce, civilization. They knew what they wanted to bring back: cotton—watered by the Blue Nile, the Zambezi River. She walked after Bryan, felt his concentration, his interest in what was before him and thought, 'In a photograph we would not look nice together.'

115 She touched the glass of a cabinet showing papyrus rolls, copper pots. She pressed her forehead and nose against the cool glass. If she could enter the cabinet, she would not make a good exhibit. She wasn't right, she was too modern, too full of mathematics.

116 Only the carpet, its petroleum blue, pleased her. She had come to this museum expecting sunlight and photographs of the Nile, something to relieve her homesickness: a comfort, a message. But the messages were not for her, not for anyone like her. A letter from West Africa, 1762, an employee to his employer in Scotland. An employee trading European goods for African curiosities. *It was difficult to make the natives understand my meaning, even by an interpreter, it being a thing so seldom asked of them, but they have all undertaken to bring something and laughed heartily at me and said, I was a good man to love their country so much . . .*

117 Love my country so much. She should not be here, there was nothing for her here. She wanted to see minarets,[5] boats fragile on the Nile, people. People like her father. The times she had sat in the waiting room of his clinic, among pregnant women, a pain in her heart because she was going to see him in a few minutes. His room, the air conditioner and the smell of his pipe, his white coat. When she hugged him, he smelled of Listerine mouthwash. He could never remember how old she was, what she was studying; six daughters, how could he keep track. In his confusion, there was freedom for her, games to play, a lot of teasing. She visited his clinic in secret, telling lies to her mother. She loved him more than she loved her mother. Her mother who did everything for her, tidied her room, sewed her clothes from *Burda* magazine. Shadia was twenty-five and her mother washed everything for her by hand, even her pants and bras.

5. **minaret** a tower in the Islamic world built specifically for the *adhan*, or call to prayer

118 'I know why they went away,' said Bryan. 'I understand why they travelled.' At last he was talking. She had not seen him intense before. He spoke in a low voice. 'They had to get away, to leave here . . .'

119 'To escape from the horrible weather . . .' She was making fun of him. She wanted to put him down. The imperialists who had humiliated her history were heroes in his eyes.

120 He looked at her. 'To escape . . .' he repeated.

121 'They went to benefit themselves,' she said, 'people go away because they benefit in some way.'

122 'I want to get away,' he said.

123 She remembered when he had opened his palms on the table and said, 'I went on a trip to Mecca.' There had been pride in his voice.

124 'I should have gone somewhere else for the course,' he went on. 'A new place, somewhere down south.'

125 He was on a plateau, not like her. She was fighting and struggling for a piece of paper that would say she was awarded an M.Sc. from a British university. For him, the course was a continuation.

126 'Come and see,' he said, and he held her arm. No one had touched her before, not since she had hugged her mother goodbye. Months now in this country and no one had touched her.

127 She pulled her arm away. She walked away, quickly up the stairs. Metal steps rattled under her feet. She ran up the stairs to the next floor. Guns, a row of guns aiming at her. They had been waiting to blow her away. Scottish arms of centuries ago, gunfire in service of the empire.

128 Silver muzzles, a dirty grey now. They must have shone prettily once, under a sun far away. If they blew her away now, where would she fly and fall? A window that looked out at the hostile sky. She shivered in spite of the wool she was wearing, layers of clothes. Hell is not only blazing fire, a part of it is freezing cold, torturous ice and snow. In Scotland's winter you have a glimpse of this unseen world, feel the breath of it in your bones.

129 There was a bench and she sat down. There was no one here on this floor. She was alone with sketches of jungle animals, words on the wall. A diplomat away from home, in Ethiopia in 1903: Asafa's country long before Asafa was born. *It is difficult to imagine anything more satisfactory or better worth taking part in than a lion drive. We rode back to camp feeling very well indeed. Archie was quite right when he said that this was the first time since we have started*

that we have really been in Africa—the real Africa of jungle inhabited only by game, and plains where herds of antelope meet your eye in every direction.

130   'Shadiya, don't cry.' He still pronounced her name wrongly because she had not told him how to say it properly.

131   He sat next to her on the bench, the blur of his navy jacket blocking the guns, the wall-length pattern of antelope herds. She should explain that she cried easily, there was no need for the alarm on his face. His awkward voice: 'Why are ye crying?'

132   He didn't know, he didn't understand. He was all wrong, not a substitute . . .

133   'They are telling lies in this museum,' she said. 'Don't believe them. It's all wrong. It's not jungles and antelopes, it's people. We have things like computers and cars. We have 7UP in Africa, and some people, a few people, have bathrooms with golden taps . . . I shouldn't be here with you. You shouldn't talk to me . . .'

134   He said, 'Museums change, I can change . . .'

135   He didn't know it was a steep path she had no strength for. He didn't understand. Many things, years and landscapes, gulfs. If she had been strong she would have explained, and not tired of explaining. She would have patiently taught him another language, letters curved like the epsilon and gamma he knew from mathematics. She would have shown him that words could be read from the right to left. If she had not been small in the museum, if she had been really strong, she would have made his trip to Mecca real, not only in a book.

From *Coloured Lights* by Leila Aboulela. © Leila Aboulela, 2001. Reproduced with permission of Birlinn Limited via PLSclear.

✏ WRITE

DISCUSSION: Divide yourselves into groups of four or five. Discuss these questions: How do Shadia and Bryan view each other? What is the main reason they find it so hard to communicate with each other? Support your ideas with textual evidence. Take notes as answers are suggested, and be prepared to share your group's notes with the rest of the class. If you have time, talk about your own experiences with cross-cultural friendships.

A Temporary Matter

FICTION
Jhumpa Lahiri
1999

Introduction

Pulitzer Prize-winner Jhumpa Lahiri (b. 1967) often writes about the intricacies of love and expectation among Indian American families. In "A Temporary Matter," a story from Lahiri's debut collection, *Interpreter of Maladies,* a couple confronts the sadness they've long avoided. After their baby is stillborn, Shoba and Shukumar's marriage changes. No longer intimate with one another, Shoba spends her days outside the house, while Shukumar barely leaves. A scheduled hour-long power outage for five consecutive evenings provides the couple with a strange gift. Instead of avoiding one another, they find themselves able to talk, using the rules of a game Shoba learned from her family in India.

"He learned not to mind the silences."

1   The notice informed them that it was a temporary matter: for five days their electricity would be cut off for one hour, beginning at eight P.M. A line had gone down in the last snowstorm, and the repairmen were going to take advantage of the milder evenings to set it right. The work would affect only the houses on the quiet tree-lined

Jhumpa Lahiri

street, within walking distance of a row of brick-faced stores and a trolley stop, where Shoba and Shukumar had lived for three years.

2   "It's good of them to warn us," Shoba conceded after reading the notice aloud, more for her own benefit than Shukumar's. She let the strap of her leather satchel, plump with files, slip from her shoulders, and left it in the hallway as she walked into the kitchen. She wore a navy blue poplin raincoat over gray sweatpants and white sneakers, looking, at thirty-three, like the type of woman she'd once claimed she would never resemble.

3   She'd come from the gym. Her cranberry lipstick was visible only on the outer reaches of her mouth, and her eyeliner had left charcoal patches beneath her lower lashes. She used to look this way sometimes, Shukumar thought, on mornings after a party or a night at a bar, when she'd been too lazy to wash her face, too eager to collapse into his arms. She dropped a sheaf of mail on the table without a glance. Her eyes were still fixed on the notice in her other hand. "But they should do this sort of thing during the day."

4   "When I'm here, you mean," Shukumar said. He put a glass lid on a pot of lamb, adjusting it so only the slightest bit of steam could escape. Since January he'd been working at home, trying to complete the final chapters of his dissertation on agrarian[1] revolts in India. "When do the repairs start?"

---

1. **agrarian** concerning the cultivation or distribution of land

5　"It says March nineteenth. Is today the nineteenth?" Shoba walked over to the framed corkboard that hung on the wall by the fridge, bare except for a calendar of William Morris wallpaper patterns. She looked at it as if for the first time, studying the wallpaper pattern carefully on the top half before allowing her eyes to fall to the numbered grid on the bottom. A friend had sent the calendar in the mail as a Christmas gift, even though Shoba and Shukumar hadn't celebrated Christmas that year.

6　"Today then," Shoba announced. "You have a dentist appointment next Friday, by the way."

7　He ran his tongue over the tops of his teeth; he'd forgotten to brush them that morning. It wasn't the first time. He hadn't left the house at all that day, or the day before. The more Shoba stayed out, the more she began putting in extra hours at work and taking on additional projects, the more he wanted to stay in, not even leaving to get the mail, or to buy fruit or wine at the stores by the trolley stop.

8　Six months ago, in September, Shukumar was at an academic conference in Baltimore when Shoba went into labor, three weeks before her due date. He hadn't wanted to go to the conference, but she had insisted; it was important to make contacts, and he would be entering the job market next year. She told him that she had his number at the hotel, and a copy of his schedule and flight numbers, and she had arranged with her friend Gillian for a ride to the hospital in the event of an emergency. When the cab pulled away that morning for the airport, Shoba stood waving good-bye in her robe, with one arm resting on the mound of her belly as if it were a perfectly natural part of her body.

9　Each time he thought of that moment, the last moment he saw Shoba pregnant, it was the cab he remembered most, a station wagon, painted red with blue lettering. It was cavernous compared to their own car. Although Shukumar was six feet tall, with hands too big ever to rest comfortably in the pockets of his jeans, he felt dwarfed in the back seat. As the cab sped down Beacon Street, he imagined a day when he and Shoba might need to buy a station wagon of their own, to cart their children back and forth from music lessons and dentist appointments. He imagined himself gripping the wheel, as Shoba turned around to hand the children juice boxes. Once, these images of parenthood had troubled Shukumar, adding to his anxiety that he was still a student at thirty-five. But that early autumn morning, the trees still heavy with bronze leaves, he welcomed the image for the first time.

10　A member of the staff had found him somehow among the identical convention rooms and handed him a stiff square of stationery. It was only a telephone number, but Shukumar knew it was the hospital. When he returned to Boston it was over. The baby had been born dead. Shoba was lying on a bed, asleep, in a private room so small there was barely enough space to stand beside her, in a wing of the hospital they hadn't been to on the tour for expectant parents. Her placenta had weakened and she'd had a cesarean,[2] though not quickly enough. The doctor explained that these things happen. He smiled in the kindest way it was possible to smile at people known only professionally. Shoba would be back on her feet in a few weeks. There was nothing to indicate that she would not be able to have children in the future.

11   These days Shoba was always gone by the time Shukumar woke up. He would open his eyes and see the long black hairs she shed on her pillow and think of her, dressed, sipping her third cup of coffee already, in her office downtown, where she searched for typographical errors in textbooks and marked them, in a code she had once explained to him, with an assortment of colored pencils. She would do the same for his dissertation, she promised, when it was ready. He envied her the specificity of her task, so unlike the elusive nature of his. He was a mediocre student who had a facility for absorbing details without curiosity. Until September he had been **diligent** if not dedicated, summarizing chapters, outlining arguments on pads of yellow lined paper. But now he would lie in their bed until he grew bored, gazing at his side of the closet which Shoba always left partly open, at the row of the tweed jackets and corduroy trousers he would not have to choose from to teach his classes that semester. After the baby died it was too late to withdraw from his teaching duties. But his adviser had arranged things so that he had the spring semester to himself. Shukumar was in his sixth year of graduate school. "That and the summer should give you a good push," his adviser had said. "You should be able to wrap things up by next September."

12   But nothing was pushing Shukumar. Instead he thought of how he and Shoba had become experts at avoiding each other in their three-bedroom house, spending as much time on separate floors as possible. He thought of how he no longer looked forward to weekends, when she sat for hours on the sofa with her colored pencils and her files, so that he feared that putting on a record in his own house might be rude. He thought of how long it had been since she looked into his eyes and smiled, or whispered his name on those rare occasions they still reached for each other's bodies before sleeping.

2. **cesarean** a cesarean section, or c-section, is a surgical procedure to deliver a baby through an incision in the abdomen

13   In the beginning he had believed that it would pass, that he and Shoba would get through it all somehow. She was only thirty-three. She was strong, on her feet again. But it wasn't a consolation. It was often nearly lunchtime when Shukumar would finally pull himself out of bed and head downstairs to the coffeepot, pouring out the extra bit Shoba left for him, along with an empty mug, on the countertop.

14   Shukumar gathered onion skins in his hands and let them drop into the garbage pail, on top of the ribbons of fat he'd trimmed from the lamb. He ran the water in the sink, soaking the knife and the cutting board, and rubbed a lemon half along his fingertips to get rid of the garlic smell, a trick he'd learned from Shoba. It was seven-thirty. Through the window he saw the sky, like soft black pitch. Uneven banks of snow still lined the sidewalks, though it was warm enough for people to walk about without hats or gloves. Nearly three feet had fallen in the last storm, so that for a week people had to walk single file, in narrow trenches. For a week that was Shukumar's excuse for not leaving the house. But now the trenches were widening, and water drained steadily into grates in the pavement.

15   "The lamb won't be done by eight," Shukumar said. "We may have to eat in the dark."

16   "We can light candles," Shoba suggested. She unclipped her hair, coiled neatly at her nape during the days, and pried the sneakers from her feet without untying them. "I'm going to shower before the lights go," she said, heading for the staircase. "I'll be down."

17   Shukumar moved her satchel and her sneakers to the side of the fridge. She wasn't this way before. She used to put her coat on a hanger, her sneakers in the closet, and she paid bills as soon as they came. But now she treated the house as if it were a hotel. The fact that the yellow chintz armchair in the living room clashed with the blue-and-maroon Turkish carpet no longer bothered her. On the enclosed porch at the back of the house, a crisp white bag still sat on the wicker chaise, filled with lace she had once planned to turn into curtains.

18   While Shoba showered, Shukumar went into the downstairs bathroom and found a new toothbrush in its box beneath the sink. The cheap, stiff bristles hurt his gums, and he spit some blood into the basin. The spare brush was one of many stored in a metal basket. Shoba had bought them once when they were on sale, in the event that a visitor decided, at the last minute, to spend the night.

19   It was typical of her. She was the type to prepare for surprises, good and bad. If she found a skirt or a purse she liked she bought two. She kept the bonuses

Please note that excerpts and passages in the StudySync® library and this workbook are intended as touchstones to generate interest in an author's work. The excerpts and passages do not substitute for the reading of entire texts, and StudySync® strongly recommends that students seek out and purchase the whole literary or informational work in order to experience it as the author intended. Links to online resellers are available in our digital library. In addition, complete works may be ordered through an authorized reseller by filling out and returning to StudySync® the order form enclosed in this workbook.

Reading & Writing Companion   81

NOTES

from her job in a separate bank account in her name. It hadn't bothered him. His own mother had fallen to pieces when his father died, abandoning the house he grew up in and moving back to Calcutta, leaving Shukumar to settle it all. He liked that Shoba was different. It astonished him, her **capacity** to think ahead. When she used to do the shopping, the pantry was always stocked with extra bottles of olive and corn oil, depending on whether they were cooking Italian or Indian. There were endless boxes of pasta in all shapes and colors, zippered sacks of basmati rice, whole sides of lambs and goats from the Muslim butchers at Haymarket, chopped up and frozen in endless plastic bags. Every other Saturday they wound through the maze of stalls Shukumar eventually knew by heart. He watched in disbelief as she bought more food, trailing behind her with canvas bags as she pushed through the crowd, arguing under the morning sun with boys too young to shave but already missing teeth, who twisted up brown paper bags of artichokes, plums, gingerroot, and yams, and dropped them on their scales, and tossed them to Shoba one by one. She didn't mind being jostled, even when she was pregnant. She was tall, and broad-shouldered, with hips that her obstetrician assured her were made for childbearing. During the drive back home, as the car curved along the Charles, they **invariably** marveled at how much food they'd bought.

20 It never went to waste. When friends dropped by, Shoba would throw together meals that appeared to have taken half a day to prepare, from things she had frozen and bottled, not cheap things in tins but peppers she had marinated herself with rosemary, and chutneys that she cooked on Sundays, stirring boiling pots of tomatoes and prunes. Her labeled mason jars lined the shelves of the kitchen, in endless sealed pyramids, enough, they'd agreed, to last for their grandchildren to taste. They'd eaten it all by now. Shukumar had been going through their supplies steadily, preparing meals for the two of them, measuring out cupfuls of rice, defrosting bags of meat day after day. He combed through her cookbooks every afternoon, following her penciled instructions to use two teaspoons of ground coriander seeds instead of one, or red lentils instead of yellow. Each of the recipes was dated, telling the first time they had eaten the dish together. April 2, cauliflower with fennel. January 14, chicken with almonds and sultanas. He had no memory of eating those meals, and yet there they were, recorded in her neat proofreader's hand. Shukumar enjoyed cooking now. It was the one thing that made him feel productive. If it weren't for him, he knew, Shoba would eat a bowl of cereal for her dinner.

21 Tonight, with no lights, they would have to eat together. For months now they'd served themselves from the stove, and he'd taken his plate into his study, letting the meal grow cold on his desk before shoving it into his mouth without pause, while Shoba took her plate to the living room and watched game shows, or proofread files with her arsenal of colored pencils at hand.

Skill:
Theme

The characters live in modern-day Boston during a week of nightly blackouts on their street. This forces them to stop avoiding each other, building suspense and suggesting a theme having to do with how relationships change.

22   At some point in the evening she visited him. When he heard her approach he would put away his novel and begin typing sentences. She would rest her hands on his shoulders and stare with him into the blue glow of the computer screen. "Don't work too hard," she would say after a minute or two, and head off to bed. It was the one time in the day she sought him out, and yet he'd come to dread it. He knew it was something she forced herself to do. She would look around the walls of the room, which they had decorated together last summer with a border of marching ducks and rabbits playing trumpets and drums. By the end of August there was a cherry crib under the window, a white changing table with mint-green knobs, and a rocking chair with checkered cushions. Shukumar had disassembled it all before bringing Shoba back from the hospital, scraping off the rabbits and ducks with a spatula. For some reason the room did not haunt him the way it haunted Shoba. In January, when he stopped working at his carrel[3] in the library, he set up his desk there deliberately, partly because the room soothed him, and partly because it was a place Shoba avoided.

23   Shukumar returned to the kitchen and began to open drawers. He tried to locate a candle among the scissors, the eggbeaters and whisks, the mortar and pestle she'd bought in a bazaar in Calcutta, and used to pound garlic cloves and cardamom pods, back when she used to cook. He found a flashlight, but no batteries, and a half-empty box of birthday candles. Shoba had thrown him a surprise birthday party last May. One hundred and twenty people had crammed into the house — all the friends and the friends of friends they now systematically avoided. Bottles of vinho verde had nested in a bed of ice in the bathtub. Shoba was in her fifth month, drinking ginger ale from a martini glass. She had made a vanilla cream cake with custard and spun sugar. All night she kept Shukumar's long fingers linked with hers as they walked among the guests at the party.

24   Since September their only guest had been Shoba's mother. She came from Arizona and stayed with them for two months after Shoba returned from the hospital. She cooked dinner every night, drove herself to the supermarket, washed their clothes, put them away. She was a religious woman. She set up a small shrine, a framed picture of a lavender-faced goddess and a plate of marigold petals, on the bedside table in the guest room, and prayed twice a day for healthy grandchildren in the future. She was polite to Shukumar without being friendly. She folded his sweaters with an expertise she had learned from her job in a department store. She replaced a missing button on his winter coat and knit him a beige and brown scarf, presenting it to him without the least bit of ceremony, as if he had only dropped it and hadn't noticed. She never talked to him about Shoba; once, when he mentioned the baby's death, she looked up from her knitting, and said, "But you weren't even there."

---

3. **carrel** a small cubicle or study area in a library

25   It struck him as odd that there were no real candles in the house. That Shoba hadn't prepared for such an ordinary emergency. He looked now for something to put the birthday candles in and settled on the soil of a potted ivy that normally sat on the windowsill over the sink. Even though the plant was inches from the tap, the soil was so dry that he had to water it first before the candles would stand straight. He pushed aside the things on the kitchen table, the piles of mail, the unread library books. He remembered their first meals there, when they were so thrilled to be married, to be living together in the same house at last, that they would just reach for each other foolishly, more eager to make love than to eat. He put down two embroidered place mats, a wedding gift from an uncle in Lucknow, and set out the plates and wineglasses they usually saved for guests. He put the ivy in the middle, the white-edged, star-shaped leaves girded by ten little candles. He switched on the digital clock radio and tuned it to a jazz station.

26   "What's all this?" Shoba said when she came downstairs. Her hair was wrapped in a thick white towel. She undid the towel and draped it over a chair, allowing her hair, damp and dark, to fall across her back. As she walked absently toward the stove she took out a few tangles with her fingers. She wore a clean pair of sweatpants, a T-shirt, an old flannel robe. Her stomach was flat again, her waist narrow before the flare of her hips, the belt of the robe tied in a floppy knot.

27   It was nearly eight. Shukumar put the rice on the table and the lentils from the night before into the microwave oven, punching the numbers on the timer.

28   "You made *rogan josh,*" Shoba observed, looking through the glass lid at the bright paprika stew.

29   Shukumar took out a piece of lamb, pinching it quickly between his fingers so as not to scald himself. He prodded a larger piece with a serving spoon to make sure the meat slipped easily from the bone. "It's ready," he announced.

30   The microwave had just beeped when the lights went out, and the music disappeared.

31   "Perfect timing," Shoba said.

32   "All I could find were birthday candles." He lit up the ivy, keeping the rest of the candles and a book of matches by his plate.

33   "It doesn't matter," she said, running a finger along the stem of her wineglass. "It looks lovely."

Copyright © BookheadEd Learning, LLC

34   In the dimness, he knew how she sat, a bit forward in her chair, ankles crossed against the lowest rung, left elbow on the table. During his search for the candles, Shukumar had found a bottle of wine in a crate he had thought was empty. He clamped the bottle between his knees while he turned in the corkscrew. He worried about spilling, and so he picked up the glasses and held them close to his lap while he filled them. They served themselves, stirring the rice with their forks, squinting as they **extracted** bay leaves and cloves from the stew. Every few minutes Shukumar lit a few more birthday candles and drove them into the soil of the pot.

35   "It's like India," Shoba said, watching him tend his makeshift candelabra. "Sometimes the current disappears for hours at a stretch. I once had to attend an entire rice ceremony[4] in the dark. The baby just cried and cried. It must have been so hot."

36   Their baby had never cried, Shukumar considered. Their baby would never have a rice ceremony, even though Shoba had already made the guest list, and decided on which of her three brothers she was going to ask to feed the child its first taste of solid food, at six months if it was a boy, seven if it was a girl.

37   "Are you hot?" he asked her. He pushed the blazing ivy pot to the other end of the table, closer to the piles of books and mail, making it even more difficult for them to see each other. He was suddenly irritated that he couldn't go upstairs and sit in front of the computer.

38   "No. It's delicious," she said, tapping her plate with her fork. "It really is."

39   He refilled the wine in her glass. She thanked him.

40   They weren't like this before. Now he had to struggle to say something that interested her, something that made her look up from her plate, or from her proofreading files. Eventually he gave up trying to amuse her. He learned not to mind the silences.

41   "I remember during power failures at my grandmother's house, we all had to say something," Shoba continued. He could barely see her face, but from her tone he knew her eyes were narrowed, as if trying to focus on a distant object. It was a habit of hers.

42   "Like what?"

43   "I don't know. A little poem. A joke. A fact about the world. For some reason my relatives always wanted me to tell them the names of my friends in

---

4. **rice ceremony** Annaprashan, the Indian ritual of a baby's first feeding with rice

America. I don't know why the information was so interesting to them. The last time I saw my aunt she asked after four girls I went to elementary school with in Tucson. I barely remember them now."

44   Shukumar hadn't spent as much time in India as Shoba had. His parents, who settled in New Hampshire, used to go back without him. The first time he'd gone as an infant he'd nearly died of amoebic dysentery. His father, a nervous type, was afraid to take him again, in case something were to happen, and left him with his aunt and uncle in Concord. As a teenager he preferred sailing camp or scooping ice cream during the summers to going to Calcutta. It wasn't until after his father died, in his last year of college, that the country began to interest him, and he studied its history from course books as if it were any other subject. He wished now that he had his own childhood story of India.

45   "Let's do that," she said suddenly.

46   "Do what?"

47   "Say something to each other in the dark."

48   "Like what? I don't know any jokes."

49   "No, no jokes." She thought for a minute. "How about telling each other something we've never told before."

50   "I used to play this game in high school," Shukumar recalled. "When I got drunk."

51   "You're thinking of truth or dare. This is different. Okay, I'll start." She took a sip of wine. "The first time I was alone in your apartment, I looked in your address book to see if you'd written me in. I think we'd known each other two weeks."

52   "Where was I?"

53   "You went to answer the telephone in the other room. It was your mother, and I figured it would be a long call. I wanted to know if you'd promoted me from the margins of your newspaper."

54   "Had I?"

55   "No. But I didn't give up on you. Now it's your turn."

56   He couldn't think of anything, but Shoba was waiting for him to speak. She hadn't appeared so determined in months. What was there left to say to her?

Copyright © BookheadEd Learning, LLC

He thought back to their first meeting, four years earlier at a lecture hall in Cambridge, where a group of Bengali poets were giving a recital. They'd ended up side by side, on folding wooden chairs. Shukumar was soon bored; he was unable to decipher the literary diction, and couldn't join the rest of the audience as they sighed and nodded solemnly after certain phrases. Peering at the newspaper folded in his lap, he studied the temperatures of cities around the world. Ninety-one degrees in Singapore yesterday, fifty-one in Stockholm. When he turned his head to the left, he saw a woman next to him making a grocery list on the back of a folder, and was startled to find that she was beautiful.

57   "Okay" he said, remembering. "The first time we went out to dinner, to the Portuguese place, I forgot to tip the waiter. I went back the next morning, found out his name, left money with the manager."

58   "You went all the way back to Somerville just to tip a waiter?"

59   "I took a cab."

60   "Why did you forget to tip the waiter?"

61   The birthday candles had burned out, but he pictured her face clearly in the dark, the wide tilting eyes, the full grape-toned lips, the fall at age two from her high chair still visible as a comma on her chin. Each day, Shukumar noticed, her beauty, which had once overwhelmed him, seemed to fade. The cosmetics that had seemed superfluous were necessary now, not to improve her but to define her somehow.

62   "By the end of the meal I had a funny feeling that I might marry you," he said, admitting it to himself as well as to her for the first time. "It must have distracted me."

63   The next night Shoba came home earlier than usual. There was lamb left over from the evening before, and Shukumar heated it up so that they were able to eat by seven. He'd gone out that day, through the melting snow, and bought a packet of taper candles from the corner store, and batteries to fit the flashlight. He had the candles ready on the countertop, standing in brass holders shaped like lotuses, but they ate under the glow of the copper-shaded ceiling lamp that hung over the table.

64   When they had finished eating, Shukumar was surprised to see that Shoba was stacking her plate on top of his, and then carrying them over to the sink. He had assumed she would retreat to the living room, behind her barricade of files.

Please note that excerpts and passages in the StudySync® library and this workbook are intended as touchstones to generate interest in an author's work. The excerpts and passages do not substitute for the reading of entire texts, and StudySync® strongly recommends that students seek out and purchase the whole literary or informational work in order to experience it as the author intended. Links to online resellers are available in our digital library. In addition, complete works may be ordered through an authorized reseller by filling out and returning to StudySync® the order form enclosed in this workbook.

Reading & Writing Companion   87

65 "Don't worry about the dishes," he said, taking them from her hands.

66 "It seems silly not to," she replied, pouring a drop of detergent onto a sponge. "It's nearly eight o'clock."

Skill:
Theme

The story is told in third-person point of view, but the narrator reveals Shukumar's thoughts. He "felt good" reflecting on memories. Sharing secrets changed him, suggesting that minor revelations can have a big impact.

67 His heart quickened. All day Shukumar had looked forward to the lights going out. He thought about what Shoba had said the night before, about looking in his address book. It felt good to remember her as she was then, how bold yet nervous she'd been when they first met, how hopeful. They stood side by side at the sink, their reflections fitting together in the frame of the window. It made him shy, the way he felt the first time they stood together in a mirror. He couldn't recall the last time they'd been photographed. They had stopped attending parties, went nowhere together. The film in his camera still contained pictures of Shoba, in the yard, when she was pregnant.

68 After finishing the dishes, they leaned against the counter, drying their hands on either end of a towel. At eight o'clock the house went black. Shukumar lit the wicks of the candles, impressed by their long, steady flames.

69 "Let's sit outside," Shoba said. "I think it's warm still."

70 They each took a candle and sat down on the steps. It seemed strange to be sitting outside with patches of snow still on the ground. But everyone was out of their houses tonight, the air fresh enough to make people restless. Screen doors opened and closed. A small parade of neighbors passed by with flashlights.

71 "We're going to the bookstore to browse," a silver-haired man called out. He was walking with his wife, a thin woman in a windbreaker, and holding a dog on a leash. They were the Bradfords, and they had tucked a sympathy card into Shoba and Shukumar's mailbox back in September. "I hear they've got their power."

72 "They'd better," Shukumar said. "Or you'll be browsing in the dark."

73 The woman laughed, slipping her arm through the crook of her husband's elbow. "Want to join us?"

74 "No thanks," Shoba and Shukumar called out together. It surprised Shukumar that his words matched hers.

75 He wondered what Shoba would tell him in the dark. The worst possibilities had already run through his head. That she'd had an affair. That she didn't respect him for being thirty-five and still a student. That she blamed him for being in Baltimore the way her mother did. But he knew those things weren't

Copyright © BookheadEd Learning, LLC

true. She'd been faithful, as had he. She believed in him. It was she who had insisted he go to Baltimore. What didn't they know about each other? He knew she curled her fingers tightly when she slept, that her body twitched during bad dreams. He knew it was honeydew she favored over cantaloupe. He knew that when they returned from the hospital the first thing she did when she walked into the house was pick out objects of theirs and toss them into a pile in the hallway: books from the shelves, plants from the windowsills, paintings from walls, photos from tables, pots and pans that hung from the hooks over the stove. Shukumar had stepped out of her way, watching as she moved **methodically** from room to room. When she was satisfied, she stood there staring at the pile she'd made, her lips drawn back in such distaste that Shukumar had thought she would spit. Then she'd started to cry.

76 He began to feel cold as he sat there on the steps. He felt that he needed her to talk first, in order to reciprocate.

77 "That time when your mother came to visit us," she said finally. "When I said one night that I had to stay late at work, I went out with Gillian and had a martini."

78 He looked at her profile, the slender nose, the slightly masculine set of her jaw. He remembered that night well; eating with his mother, tired from teaching two classes back to back, wishing Shoba were there to say more of the right things because he came up with only the wrong ones. It had been twelve years since his father had died, and his mother had come to spend two weeks with him and Shoba, so they could honor his father's memory together. Each night his mother cooked something his father had liked, but she was too upset to eat the dishes herself, and her eyes would well up as Shoba stroked her hand. "It's so touching," Shoba had said to him at the time. Now he pictured Shoba with Gillian, in a bar with striped velvet sofas, the one they used to go to after the movies, making sure she got her extra olive, asking Gillian for a cigarette. He imagined her complaining, and Gillian sympathizing about visits from in-laws. It was Gillian who had driven Shoba to the hospital.

79 "Your turn," she said, stopping his thoughts.

80 At the end of their street Shukumar heard sounds of a drill and the electricians shouting over it. He looked at the darkened facades of the houses lining the street. Candles glowed in the windows of one. In spite of the warmth, smoke rose from the chimney.

81 "I cheated on my Oriental Civilization exam in college," he said. "It was my last semester, my last set of exams. My father had died a few months before. I could see the blue book of the guy next to me. He was an American guy, a

Please note that excerpts and passages in the StudySync® library and this workbook are intended as touchstones to generate interest in an author's work. The excerpts and passages do not substitute for the reading of entire texts, and StudySync® strongly recommends that students seek out and purchase the whole literary or informational work in order to experience it as the author intended. Links to online resellers are available in our digital library. In addition, complete works may be ordered through an authorized reseller by filling out and returning to StudySync® the order form enclosed in this workbook.

Reading & Writing Companion 89

NOTES

maniac. He knew Urdu and Sanskrit. I couldn't remember if the verse we had to identify was an example of a *ghazal* or not. I looked at his answer and copied it down."

82   It had happened over fifteen years ago. He felt relief now, having told her.

83   She turned to him, looking not at his face, but at his shoes—old moccasins he wore as if they were slippers, the leather at the back permanently flattened. He wondered if it bothered her, what he'd said. She took his hand and pressed it. "You didn't have to tell me why you did it," she said, moving closer to him.

84   They sat together until nine o'clock, when the lights came on. They heard some people across the street clapping from their porch, and televisions being turned on. The Bradfords walked back down the street, eating ice-cream cones and waving. Shoba and Shukumar waved back. Then they stood up, his hand still in hers, and went inside.

85   Somehow, without saying anything, it had turned into this. Into an exchange of confessions—the little ways they'd hurt or disappointed each other, and themselves. The following day Shukumar thought for hours about what to say to her. He was torn between admitting that he once ripped out a photo of a woman in one of the fashion magazines she used to subscribe to and carried it in his books for a week, or saying that he really hadn't lost the sweater-vest she bought him for their third wedding anniversary but had exchanged it for cash at Filene's, and that he had gotten drunk alone in the middle of the day at a hotel bar. For their first anniversary, Shoba had cooked a ten-course dinner just for him. The vest depressed him. "My wife gave me a sweater-vest for our anniversary," he complained to the bartender, his head heavy with cognac. "What do you expect?" the bartender had replied. "You're married."

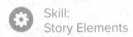

Skill:
Story Elements

Shukumar feels disconnected from Shoba, but instead of talking to her about it, he fixates on a picture from a magazine. This dilemma shows that the conflict between the characters had already been brewing before the baby's death.

86   As for the picture of the woman, he didn't know why he'd ripped it out. She wasn't as pretty as Shoba. She wore a white sequined dress, and had a sullen face and lean, mannish legs. Her bare arms were raised, her fists around her head, as if she were about to punch herself in the ears. It was an advertisement for stockings. Shoba had been pregnant at the time, her stomach suddenly immense, to the point where Shukumar no longer wanted to touch her. The first time he saw the picture he was lying in bed next to her, watching her as she read. When he noticed the magazine in the recycling pile he found the woman and tore out the page as carefully as he could. For about a week he allowed himself a glimpse each day. He felt an intense desire for the woman, but it was a desire that turned to disgust after a minute or two. It was the closest he'd come to infidelity.

87　He told Shoba about the sweater on the third night, the picture on the fourth. She said nothing as he spoke, expressed no protest or reproach. She simply listened, and then she took his hand, pressing it as she had before. On the third night, she told him that once after a lecture they'd attended, she let him speak to the chairman of his department without telling him that he had a dab of pâté on his chin. She'd been irritated with him for some reason, and so she'd let him go on and on, about securing his fellowship for the following semester, without putting a finger to her own chin as a signal. The fourth night, she said that she never liked the one poem he'd ever published in his life, in a literary magazine in Utah. He'd written the poem after meeting Shoba. She added that she found the poem sentimental.

88　Something happened when the house was dark. They were able to talk to each other again. The third night after supper they'd sat together on the sofa, and once it was dark he began kissing her awkwardly on her forehead and her face, though it was dark he closed his eyes, and knew that she did, too. The fourth night they walked carefully upstairs, to bed, feeling together for the final step with their feet before the landing, and making love with a desperation they had forgotten. She wept without sound, and whispered his name, and traced his eyebrows with her finger in the dark. As he made love to her he wondered what he would say to her the next night, and what she would say, the thought of it exciting him. "Hold me," he said, "hold me in your arms." By the time the lights came back on downstairs, they'd fallen asleep.

89　The morning of the fifth night Shukumar found another notice from the electric company in the mailbox. The line had been repaired ahead of schedule, it said. He was disappointed. He had planned on making shrimp *malai* for Shoba, but when he arrived at the store he didn't feel like cooking anymore. It wasn't the same, he thought, knowing that the lights wouldn't go out. In the store the shrimp looked gray and thin. The coconut milk tin was dusty and overpriced. Still, he bought them, along with a beeswax candle and two bottles of wine.

90　She came home at seven-thirty. "I suppose this is the end of our game," he said when he saw her reading the notice.

91　She looked at him. "You can still light candles if you want." She hadn't been to the gym tonight. She wore a suit beneath the raincoat. Her makeup had been retouched recently.

92　When she went upstairs to change, Shukumar poured himself some wine and put on a record, a Thelonious Monk album he knew she liked.

93   When she came downstairs they ate together. She didn't thank him or compliment him. They simply ate in a darkened room, in the glow of a beeswax candle. They had survived a difficult time. They finished off the shrimp. They finished off the first bottle of wine and moved on to the second. They sat together until the candle had nearly burned away. She shifted in her chair, and Shukumar thought that she was about to say something. But instead she blew out the candle, stood up, turned on the light switch, and sat down again.

94   "Shouldn't we keep the lights off?" Shukumar asked. She set her plate aside and clasped her hands on the table. "I want you to see my face when I tell you this," she said gently.

95   His heart began to pound. The day she told him she was pregnant, she had used the very same words, saying them in the same gentle way, turning off the basketball game he'd been watching on television. He hadn't been prepared then. Now he was.

96   Only he didn't want her to be pregnant again. He didn't want to have to pretend to be happy.

97   "I've been looking for an apartment and I've found one," she said, narrowing her eyes on something, it seemed, behind his left shoulder. It was nobody's fault, she continued. They'd been through enough. She needed some time alone. She had money saved up for a security deposit. The apartment was on Beacon Hill, so she could walk to work. She had signed the lease that night before coming home.

98   She wouldn't look at him, but he stared at her. It was obvious that she'd rehearsed the lines. All this time she'd been looking for an apartment, testing the water pressure, asking a Realtor if heat and hot water were included in the rent. It sickened Shukumar, knowing that she had spent these past evenings preparing for a life without him. He was relieved and yet he was sickened. This was what she'd been trying to tell him for the past four evenings. This was the point of her game.

99   Now it was his turn to speak. There was something he'd sworn he would never tell her, and for six months he had done his best to block it from his mind. Before the ultrasound she had asked the doctor not to tell her the sex of their child, and Shukumar had agreed. She had wanted it to be a surprise.

100   Later, those few times they talked about what had happened, she said at least they'd been spared that knowledge. In a way she almost took pride in her decision, for it enabled her to seek refuge in a mystery. He knew that she assumed it was a mystery for him, too. He'd arrived too late from Baltimore—when it was all over and she was lying on the hospital bed. But

Skill:
Story Elements

Shukumar has to decide whether or not to tell Shoba the sex of their baby. He wanted to protect Shoba, but now that she has hurt him, he wants to hurt her back. The motivation to cause Shoba pain leads to the climax of the story.

he hadn't. He'd arrived early enough to see their baby, and to hold him before they cremated him. At first he had recoiled at the suggestion, but the doctor said holding the baby might help him with the process of grieving. Shoba was asleep. The baby had been cleaned off, his bulbous lids shut tight to the world.

101 "Our baby was a boy," he said. "His skin was more red than brown. He had black hair on his head. He weighed almost five pounds. His fingers were curled shut, just like yours in the night."

102 Shoba looked at him now, her face contorted with sorrow. He had cheated on a college exam, ripped a picture of a woman out of a magazine. He had returned a sweater and got drunk in the middle of the day instead. These were the things he had told her. He had held his son, who had known life only within her, against his chest in a darkened room in an unknown wing of the hospital. He had held him until a nurse knocked and took him away, and he promised himself that day that he would never tell Shoba, because he still loved her then, and it was the one thing in her life that she had wanted to be a surprise.

103 Shukumar stood up and stacked his plate on top of hers. He carried the plates to the sink, but instead of running the tap he looked out the window. Outside the evening was still warm, and the Bradfords were walking arm in arm. As he watched the couple the room went dark, and he spun around. Shoba had turned the lights off. She came back to the table and sat down, and after a moment Shukumar joined her. They wept together, for the things they now knew.

"A Temporary Matter" from INTERPRETER OF MALADIES by Jhumpa Lahiri. Copyright © 1999 by Jhumpa Lahiri. Reprinted by permission of Houghton Mifflin Harcourt Publishing Company. All rights reserved.

Please note that excerpts and passages in the StudySync® library and this workbook are intended as touchstones to generate interest in an author's work. The excerpts and passages do not substitute for the reading of entire texts, and StudySync® strongly recommends that students seek out and purchase the whole literary or informational work in order to experience it as the author intended. Links to online resellers are available in our digital library. In addition, complete works may be ordered through an authorized reseller by filling out and returning to StudySync® the order form enclosed in this workbook.

Reading & Writing Companion 93

A Temporary Matter

First Read

Read the short story "A Temporary Matter." After you read, complete the Think Questions below.

☁ THINK QUESTIONS

1. How does Shukumar feel about himself? Why? Cite evidence from the story to support your answer.

2. What new habits do Shoba and Shukumar develop after the death of their baby, and what do these habits reveal about their relationship? Cite evidence from the story to support your answer.

3. How did Shukumar feel about Shoba before the death of their baby? What evidence from the text leads you to this conclusion?

4. Use context clues to determine the meaning of the word **diligent** as it is used in "A Temporary Matter." Write your definition of *diligent* here, and explain which clues helped you determine its meaning.

5. Keeping in mind that the Latin prefix *ex-* means "from" and that the Latin root *tract* means "to draw or pull," determine the meaning of the word **extracted** as it is used in "A Temporary Matter." Write your definition of *extract* here, and explain which clues helped you decide on its meaning.

Skill:
Theme

Use the Checklist to analyze Theme in "A Temporary Matter." Refer to the sample student annotations about Theme in the text.

••• CHECKLIST FOR THEME

To identify two or more themes or central ideas of a text, note the following:

- ✓ the subject and how it relates to the themes in the text

- ✓ if one or more themes is stated directly in the text

- ✓ details in the text that help reveal each theme:

  - the title and chapter headings
  - details about the setting
  - the narrator's or speaker's tone
  - characters' thoughts, actions, and dialogue
  - the central conflict, climax, and resolution of the conflict
  - shifts in characters, setting, or plot events

- ✓ when the themes interact with each other

To determine two or more themes or central ideas of a text, including how they interact and build on one another to produce a complex account, and analyze their development over the course of the text, consider the following questions:

- ✓ What are the themes in the text? When do they emerge?

- ✓ How does each theme develop over the course of the text?

- ✓ How do the themes interact and build on one another?

Skill:
Theme

Reread paragraphs 94–99 of "A Temporary Matter." Then use the Checklist on the previous page to answer the multiple-choice questions below.

↻ YOUR TURN

1. Which statement best analyzes the theme that is revealed by details like characters' thoughts, setting, and narrator's tone in this passage?

   ○ A. The change in the setting creates a homey feeling that becomes a safe space for Shoba to reveal her subjective point of view and prepares readers for the story's happy ending.

   ○ B. The shift in point of view from Shukumar's thoughts to Shoba's point of view jars the reader, mirroring the abrupt change in focus from present to past events.

   ○ C. The story's surprise ending is foreshadowed by the narrator's revelation of Shukumar's secret, which takes readers from the couple's home to a hospital.

   ○ D. The third-person limited point of view helps readers understand Shukumar's reaction to learning the truth, which is heightened by the sudden change from darkness to light.

2. This question has two parts. First, answer Part A. Then, answer Part B.

   Part A: Which theme is strongly suggested by details like characterization, setting, point of view, and plot events in this passage?

   ○ A. People rarely keep secrets.
   ○ B. You cannot hide from the truth.
   ○ C. Bad news hurts less when revealed slowly.
   ○ D. Spouses sometimes need to lie to each other.

   Part B: Which evidence best supports the answer chosen in Part A?

   ○ A. "Before the ultrasound she had asked the doctor not to tell her the sex of their child . . ."

   ○ B. "'Shouldn't we keep the lights off?' Shukumar asked. She set her plate aside and clasped her hands on the table. 'I want you to see my face when I tell you this,' she said gently."

   ○ C. "He was relieved and yet he was sickened. This was what she'd been trying to tell him for the past four evenings."

   ○ D. ". . . and for six months he had done his best to block it from his mind."

Skill:
Story Elements

Use the Checklist to analyze Story Elements in "A Temporary Matter." Refer to the sample student annotations about Story Elements in the text.

••• CHECKLIST FOR STORY ELEMENTS

To identify the impact of the author's choices regarding how to develop and relate elements of a story or drama, note the following:

- ✓ where and when the story takes place, who the main characters are, and the main conflict, or problem, in the plot

- ✓ the order of the action

- ✓ how the author introduces and develops the characters

- ✓ the impact the author's choice of setting has on the characters and their attempt to solve the problem

- ✓ the point of view the author uses, and how this shapes what readers know about the characters in the story

To analyze the impact of the author's choices regarding how to develop and relate elements of a story or drama, consider the following questions:

- ✓ How does the author's choices affect the story elements? The development of the plot?

- ✓ How does the setting influence the characters?

- ✓ Which elements of the setting impact the plot, and in particular, the problem the characters face and must solve?

- ✓ Do any flashbacks or other story elements have an effect on the development of events in the plot? How does the author's choice of utilizing a flashback affect this development?

- ✓ How does the author introduce and develop characters in the story? Why do you think the author makes these choices?

Please note that excerpts and passages in the StudySync® library and this workbook are intended as touchstones to generate interest in an author's work. The excerpts and passages do not substitute for the reading of entire texts, and StudySync® strongly recommends that students seek out and purchase the whole literary or informational work in order to experience it as the author intended. Links to online resellers are available in our digital library. In addition, complete works may be ordered through an authorized reseller by filling out and returning to StudySync® the order form enclosed in this workbook.

Reading & Writing Companion   97

Skill:
Story Elements

Reread paragraph 85 of "A Temporary Matter." Then use the Checklist on the previous page to answer the multiple-choice questions below.

↻ YOUR TURN

1. The narrator reveals that Shukumar originally lies to Shoba about what really happened to the sweater-vest because—

   ○ A. he wants Shoba to feel embarrassed about the gift.
   ○ B. he knows that Shoba would want to share the money.
   ○ C. he thinks the truth would make Shoba hurt or angry.
   ○ D. he thinks it is funny to lie to Shoba about small things.

2. How does Shukumar's decision to tell Shoba the truth affect the plot of the story?

   ○ A. It shows that Shukumar is becoming more willing to talk about difficult things with his wife.
   ○ B. It reveals that Shukumar is unloving and does not care how the truth might affect Shoba.
   ○ C. It foreshadows that Shoba may do something that will be hurtful to her husband.
   ○ D. It indicates that Shukumar regrets marrying Shoba and staying married to her.

Close Read

A Temporary Matter

Reread "A Temporary Matter." As you reread, complete the Skills Focus questions below. Then use your answers and annotations from the questions to help you complete the Write activity.

SKILLS FOCUS

1. Identify a passage in which the third-person narrator reveals Shukumar's perspective on how the characters' daily lives have changed after the death of their child. Explain how this passage develops a theme relating to changing relationships.

2. Highlight a section of the text that describes Shoba's behavior before the death of their child. Explain how the description of this behavior contributes to the reader's understanding of Shoba's character and contributes to the plot of the story.

3. Identify details that show how the setting affects characterization. Explain which details you think are particularly effective in developing a character and why.

4. In varied ways, "Love After Love," "The Museum," and "A Temporary Matter" all explore a sense of self-realization at the end of a relationship. Identify an example of a character's experiencing a moment of reflective insight in "A Temporary Matter," and compare it with a similar insight in "Love After Love" or "The Museum."

5. What effect does a change in routine have on the characters in "A Temporary Matter"? Does it cause them to change? Or does it help them realize that change has already happened?

WRITE

LITERARY ANALYSIS: Critic Christopher Tayler once described Jhumpa Lahiri's stories in this way: "Unflashily written, long, almost grave in tone, her new stories patiently accumulate detail, only gradually building up a powerful emotional charge." Do you agree that "A Temporary Matter" is like this? Examine the traits named, and find passages in the story that either prove or contradict Tayler's opinion.

Please note that excerpts and passages in the StudySync® library and this workbook are intended as touchstones to generate interest in an author's work. The excerpts and passages do not substitute for the reading of entire texts, and StudySync® strongly recommends that students seek out and purchase the whole literary or informational work in order to experience it as the author intended. Links to online resellers are available in our digital library. In addition, complete works may be ordered through an authorized reseller by filling out and returning to StudySync® the order form enclosed in this workbook.

Reading & Writing Companion

99

Commencement Address at Wellesley College

INFORMATIONAL TEXT
Chimamanda Ngozi Adichie
2015

Introduction

Nigerian-born author Chimamanda Ngozi Adichie (b. 1977) is a highly acclaimed novelist, short story writer, and critic whose advocacy on behalf of gender equality was first introduced to mass audiences in the 2013 Beyoncé song "Flawless," which samples an Adichie speech entitled "We Should All Be Feminists." In this commencement address to the 2015 graduating class of Wellesley College—a women's college in Massachusetts—Adichie outlines the unprecedented challenges and opportunities young women encounter in society today.

"That degree, and the experience of being here, is a privilege. Don't let it blind you too often."

NOTES

1 Hello class of 2015.

2 Congratulations! And thank you for that wonderful welcome. And thank you President Bottomly for that wonderful introduction.

3 I have admired Wellesley—its mission, its story, its successes—for a long time and I thank you very much for inviting me.

4 You are ridiculously lucky to be graduating from this bastion of excellence and on these beautiful acres.

5 I'm truly, truly happy to be here today, so happy, in fact, that when I found out your class color was yellow, I decided I would wear yellow eyeshadow. But on second thoughts, I realized that as much as I admire Wellesley, even yellow eyeshadow was a bit too much of a gesture. So I dug out this yellow—yellowish—headwrap instead.

6 Speaking of eyeshadow, I wasn't very interested in makeup until I was in my twenties, which is when I began to wear makeup. Because of a man. A loud, unpleasant man. He was one of the guests at a friend's dinner party. I was also a guest. I was about 23, but people often told me I looked 12. The conversation at dinner was about traditional Igbo culture, about the custom that allows only men to break the kola nut,[1] and the kola nut is a deeply symbolic part of Igbo cosmology.[2]

7 I argued that it would be better if that honor were based on achievement rather than **gender,** and he looked at me and said, dismissively, "You don't know what you are talking about, you're a small girl."

8 I wanted him to disagree with the substance of my argument, but by looking at me, young and female, it was easy for him to dismiss what I said. So I decided to try to look older.

---

1. **kola nut** fruit of the kola tree, used in beverages, gum, medicine, and religious practices of West Africa
2. **cosmology** study of the universe, its foundations and physics

9   So I thought lipstick might help. And eyeliner.

10   And I am grateful to that man because I have since come to love makeup, and its wonderful possibilities for temporary transformation.

11   So, I have not told you this anecdote as a way to illustrate my discovery of gender injustice. If anything, it's really just an ode to makeup.

12   It's really just to say that this, your graduation, is a good time to buy some lipsticks—if makeup is your sort of thing—because a good shade of lipstick can always put you in a slightly better mood on dark days.

13   It's not about my discovering gender injustice because of course I had discovered years before then. From childhood. From watching the world.

14   I already knew that the world does not extend to women the many small courtesies that it extends to men.

15   I also knew that victimhood is not a virtue. That being **discriminated** against does not make you somehow morally better.

16   And I knew that men were not inherently bad or evil. They were merely privileged.[3] And I knew that privilege blinds because it is the nature of privilege to blind.

17   I knew from this personal experience, from the class privilege I had of growing up in an educated family, that it sometimes blinded me, that I was not always as alert to the nuances of people who were different from me.

18   And you, because you now have your beautiful Wellesley degree, have become privileged, no matter what your background. That degree, and the experience of being here, is a privilege. Don't let it blind you too often. Sometimes you will need to push it aside in order to see clearly.

• • •

19   I bring greetings to you from my mother. She's a big admirer of Wellesley, and she wishes she could be here. She called me yesterday to ask how the speech-writing was going and to tell me to remember to use a lot of lotion on my legs today so they would not look ashy.

20   My mother is 73 and she retired as the first female registrar of the University of Nigeria—which was quite a big deal at the time.

---

3. **privileged** in possession of rights or advantages not accessible to everyone

21 My mother likes to tell a story of the first university meeting she chaired. It was in a large conference room, and at the head of the table was a sign that said CHAIRMAN. My mother was about to get seated there when a clerk came over and made to remove the sign. All the past meetings had of course been chaired by men, and somebody had forgotten to replace the CHAIRMAN with a new sign that said CHAIRPERSON. The clerk apologized and told her he would find the new sign, since she was not a chairman.

22 My mother said no. Actually, she said, she WAS a chairman. She wanted the sign left exactly where it was. The meeting was about to begin. She didn't want anybody to think that what she was doing in that meeting at that time on that day was in any way different from what a CHAIRMAN would have done.

23 I always liked this story, and admired what I thought of as my mother's fiercely feminist choice. I once told the story to a friend, a card-carrying feminist, and I expected her to say bravo to my mother, but she was troubled by it.

24 "Why would your mother want to be called a chairman, as though she needed the MAN part to validate her?" my friend asked.

25 In some ways, I saw my friend's point.

26 Because if there were a Standard Handbook published annually by the Secret Society of Certified Feminists, then that handbook would certainly say that a woman should not be called, nor want to be called, a CHAIRMAN.

27 But gender is always about context and **circumstance.**

28 If there is a lesson in this anecdote, apart from just telling you a story about my mother to make her happy that I spoke about her at Wellesley, then it is this: Your standardized **ideologies** will not always fit your life. Because life is messy.

. . .

29 When I was growing up in Nigeria I was expected, as every student who did well was expected, to become a doctor. Deep down I knew that what I really wanted to do was to write stories. But I did what I was supposed to do and I went into medical school.

30 I told myself that I would tough it out and become a psychiatrist and that way I could use my patients' stories for my fiction.

31 But after one year of medical school I fled. I realized I would be a very unhappy doctor and I really did not want to be responsible for the inadvertent death of

Please note that excerpts and passages in the StudySync® library and this workbook are intended as touchstones to generate interest in an author's work. The excerpts and passages do not substitute for the reading of entire texts, and StudySync® strongly recommends that students seek out and purchase the whole literary or informational work in order to experience it as the author intended. Links to online resellers are available in our digital library. In addition, complete works may be ordered through an authorized reseller by filling out and returning to StudySync® the order form enclosed in this workbook.

Reading & Writing Companion   103

NOTES

my patients. Leaving medical school was a very unusual decision, especially in Nigeria where it is very difficult to get into medical school.

32 Later, people told me that it had been very courageous of me, but I did not feel courageous at all.

33 What I felt then was not courage but a desire to make an effort. To try. I could either stay and study something that was not right for me. Or I could try and do something different. I decided to try. I took the American exams and got a scholarship to come to the US where I could study something else that was NOT related to medicine. Now it might not have worked out. I might not have been given an American scholarship.

34 My writing might not have ended up being successful. But the point is that I tried.

35 We can not always bend the world into the shapes we want but we can try, we can make a concerted and real and true effort. And you are privileged that, because of your education here, you have already been given many of the tools that you will need to try. Always just try. Because you never know.

36 And so as you graduate, as you deal with your excitement and your doubts today, I urge you to try and create the world you want to live in.

37 Minister to the world in a way that can change it. Minister radically in a real, active, practical, get your hands dirty way.

38 Wellesley will open doors for you. Walk through those doors and make your strides long and firm and sure.

39 Write television shows in which female strength is not depicted as remarkable but merely normal.

40 Teach your students to see that vulnerability is a HUMAN rather than a FEMALE trait.

41 Commission magazine articles that teach men HOW TO KEEP A WOMAN HAPPY. Because there are already too many articles that tell women how to keep a man happy. And in media interviews make sure fathers are asked how they balance family and work. In this age of 'parenting as guilt,' please spread the guilt equally. Make fathers feel as bad as mothers. Make fathers share in the glory of guilt.

42 Campaign and agitate for paid paternity leave everywhere in America.

43 Hire more women where there are few. But remember that a woman you hire doesn't have to be exceptionally good. Like a majority of the men who get hired, she just needs to be good enough.

. . .

44 Recently a feminist organization kindly nominated me for an important prize in a country that will remain unnamed. I was very pleased. I've been fortunate to have received a few prizes so far and I quite like them especially when they come with shiny presents. To get this prize, I was required to talk about how important a particular European feminist woman writer had been to me. Now the truth was that I had never managed to finish this feminist writer's book. It did not speak to me. It would have been a lie to claim that she had any major influence on my thinking. The truth is that I learned so much more about feminism from watching the women traders in the market in Nsukka where I grew up than from reading any **seminal** feminist text. I could have said that this woman was important to me, and I could have talked the talk, and I could have been given the prize and a shiny present.

45 But I didn't.

46 Because I had begun to ask myself what it really means to wear this FEMINIST label so publicly.

47 Just as I asked myself after excerpts of my feminism speech were used in a song by a talented musician whom I think some of you might know. I thought it was a very good thing that the word 'feminist' would be introduced to a new generation.

48 But I was startled by how many people, many of whom were academics, saw something troubling, even menacing, in this.

49 It was as though feminism was supposed to be an elite little cult, with esoteric rites of membership.

50 But it shouldn't. Feminism should be an inclusive party. Feminism should be a party full of different feminisms.

51 And so, class of 2015, please go out there and make Feminism a big raucous inclusive party.

. . .

52 The past three weeks have been the most emotionally difficult of my life. My father is 83 years old, a retired professor of statistics, a lovely kind man. I am an absolute Daddy's girl. Three weeks ago, he was kidnapped near his home

Copyright © Bookhead Learning, LLC

in Nigeria. And for a number of days, my family and I went through the kind of emotional pain that I have never known in my life. We were talking to threatening strangers on the phone, begging and negotiating for my father's safety and we were not always sure if my father was alive. He was released after we paid a ransom. He is well, in fairly good shape and in his usual lovely way, is very keen to reassure us all that he is fine.

53 I am still not sleeping well, I still wake up many times at night, in panic, worried that something else has gone wrong, I still cannot look at my father without fighting tears, without feeling this profound relief and gratitude that he is safe, but also rage that he had to undergo such an indignity to his body and to his spirit.

54 And the experience has made me rethink many things, what truly matters, and what doesn't. What I value, and what I don't.

55 And as you graduate today, I urge you to think about that a little more. Think about what really matters to you. Think about what you WANT to really matter to you.

56 I read about your rather lovely tradition of referring to older students as "big sisters" and younger ones as "little sisters." And I read about the rather strange thing about being thrown into the pond—and I didn't really get that—but I would very much like to be your honorary big sister today.

57 Which means that I would like to give you bits of advice as your big sister:

58 All over the world, girls are raised to make themselves likeable, to twist themselves into shapes that suit other people.

59 Please do not twist yourself into shapes to please. Don't do it. If someone likes that version of you, that version of you that is false and holds back, then they actually just like that twisted shape, and not you. And the world is such a gloriously multifaceted, diverse place that there are people in the world who will like you, the real you, as you are.

60 I am lucky that my writing has given me a platform that I choose to use to talk about things that I care about, and I have said a few things that have not been so popular with a number of people. I have been told to shut up about certain things—such as my position on the equal rights of gay people on the continent of Africa, such as my deeply held belief that men and women are completely equal. I don't speak to provoke. I speak because I think our time on earth is short and each moment that we are not our truest selves, each moment we pretend to be what we are not, each moment we say what we do not mean because we imagine that is what somebody wants us to say, then we are wasting our time on earth.

61 I don't mean to sound precious but please don't waste your time on earth, but there is one exception. The only acceptable way of wasting your time on earth is online shopping.

62 Okay, one last thing about my mother. My mother and I do not agree on many things regarding gender. There are certain things my mother believes a person should do, for the simple reason that said person 'is a woman.' Such as nod occasionally and smile even when smiling is the last thing one wants to do. Such as strategically give in to certain arguments, especially when arguing with a non-female. Such as get married and have children. I can think of fairly good reasons for doing any of these. But 'because you are a woman' is not one of them. And so, Class of 2015, never ever accept 'Because You Are A Woman' as a reason for doing or not doing anything.

63 And, finally I would like to end with a final note on the most important thing in the world: love.

64 Now girls are often raised to see love only as giving. Women are praised for their love when that love is an act of giving. But to love is to give AND to take.

65 Please love by giving and by taking. Give and be given. If you are only giving and not taking, you'll know. You'll know from that small and true voice inside you that we females are so often socialized to silence.

66 Don't silence that voice. Dare to take.

67 Congratulations.

Please note that excerpts and passages in the StudySync® library and this workbook are intended as touchstones to generate interest in an author's work. The excerpts and passages do not substitute for the reading of entire texts, and StudySync® strongly recommends that students seek out and purchase the whole literary or informational work in order to experience it as the author intended. Links to online resellers are available in our digital library. In addition, complete works may be ordered through an authorized reseller by filling out and returning to StudySync® the order form enclosed in this workbook.

Reading & Writing Companion 107

WRITE

PERSONAL RESPONSE: In her speech, Chimamanda Ngozi Adichie uses personal memories and stories to explain how small gestures of resistance (wearing makeup or wanting to be called a "chairman" instead of "chairperson," for example) have helped her and her mother be true to themselves, notwithstanding other people's attempts to transform them into something they are not. Think about your own identity. Has anyone ever pushed you to be something other than your true self? Write a brief speech that describes this situation and the outcome. Were you able to remain true to yourself, or did you have to compromise? Why is it important to be true to yourself? Why is it important for others to acknowledge your true self? (If you have never experienced such a situation, imagine one and write your speech based on that.)

Commencement Address at The New School

ARGUMENTATIVE TEXT
Zadie Smith
2014

Introduction

Novelist and essayist Zadie Smith (b. 1975) was born and raised in London, daughter of a Jamaican mother and a white English father. Her first novel, *White Teeth*, published in 2000 when she was just 25 years old, was an international sensation, frequently appearing on lists of the best British novels of the last 50 years. In her commencement address to the 2014 graduates of the New School in New York City, she underlines the power and fulfillment of public participation over private isolation.

"Be thankful you get to walk so close to other humans. It's a privilege."

Skill:
Summarizing

Zadie Smith speaks to the 2014 graduates of The New School. To understand how they feel, she will rely on how she felt as a recent college graduate seventeen years earlier.

1   Welcome graduating class of 2014 and congratulations. You did it! You made it! How do you feel?

2   I guess I can only hazard a guess which means thinking back to my own graduation in England in 1997, and extrapolate from it. Did I feel like you? I should say first that some elements of the day were rather different. I wasn't in a stadium listening to a speech. I was in an eighteenth-century hall, kneeling before the dean who spoke Latin and held one of my fingers. Don't ask me why.

3   Still the essential facts were the same.

4   Like you I was finally with my degree and had made of myself—a graduate. Like you I now had two families, the old boring one that raised me, and an exciting new one consisting of a bunch of freaks I'd met in college.

5   But part of the delightful anxiety of graduation day was trying to find a way to blend these two tribes, with their differing haircuts and political views, and hygiene standards and tastes in music. I felt like a character in two different movies. And so old! I really believed I was ancient. Impossibly distant in experience from the freshmen only three years below. I was as likely to befriend a squirrel as a freshman. Which strange relationship with time is perhaps unique to graduates and toddlers. Nowadays, at age 38, if I meet somebody who's 41, I don't **conclude** that friendship is impossible between us. But when I was 21, the gap between me and an 18-year-old felt insurmountable. Just like my four-year-old daughter, who'd rather eat sand than have a playdate with a one-year-old.

6   And what else? Oh the love dramas. So many love dramas. Mine, other people's. They take up such a large part of college life it seems unfair not to have them properly reflected in the transcript. Any full account of my university years should include the fact that I majored in English literature, with a minor in drunken discussions about the difference between loving someone and being 'in love' with that person. What can I tell you, it was the '90s. We were really into ourselves. We were into self-curation. In the '90s, we even had a thing called 'Year of Trousers' which signified any kind of ethnic or exotic

pants one brought back home from a distant (ideally third world) country. And these trousers were meant to alert to a passing stranger the fact that we'd been somewhere fascinating, and thus added further colour to our unique personalities.

7   Personally I couldn't afford the year off but I was very compelled by those trousers.

8   In short, the thing I wanted most in the world was to be an **individual.** I thought that's what my graduation signified, that I had gone from being one of the many, to one of the few. To one of the ones who would have 'choices' in life. After all my father didn't have many choices, his father had none at all. Unlike them, I had gone to university. I was a special individual. Looking back it's easy to diagnose a case of self-love. People are always accusing students of self-love, or self obsession. And this is a bit confusing because college surely encourages the habit. You concentrate on yourself in order to improve yourself. Isn't that the whole idea? And out of this process hopefully emerge strikingly competent individuals, with high self esteem, prepared for personal achievement.

9   When we graduate, though, things can get a little complicated. For how are we meant to think of this fabulous person, we've taken such care of creating? If university made me special did that mean I was worth more than my father, more than his father before him?

10   Did it mean I should expect more from life than them? Did I deserve more?

11   What does it really mean to be one of 'the few'?

12   Are the fruits of our education a sort of gift, to be circulated generously through the world, or are we to think of ourselves as pure **commodity,** on sale to the highest bidder? Well let's be honest, you're probably feeling pulled in several directions right now. And that's perfectly natural.

Skill:
Summarizing

Smith explains the choice her generation faced after college: make money by working at a bank or help others. Smith now thinks that choice is funny, which means she no longer believes what she once did.

13   In the '90s, the post-graduation dilemma was usually presented to us as a straight ethical choice, between working for the banks, and doing selfless charitable work. The comic extremity of the choice I now see was perfectly deliberate. It meant you didn't have to take it too seriously. And so we peeled off from each other. Some of us, many of us, joined the banks. But those that didn't had no special cause to pat ourselves on the back. With rare exceptions, we all pursued self interest more or less. It wasn't a surprise. We'd been raised that way. Born in the seventies, we did not live through austerity, did not go to war like my father, or his father. For the most part we did not join large political or ideological movements. We simply inherited the advantages for which a previous generation had fought.

NOTES

14 And the thing that so many of us feared was the idea of being subsumed back into the collective from which we'd come. Of being returned to the world of the many. Or doing any work at all in that world.

15 In my case this new attitude was particularly noticeable. My own mother was a social worker, and I had teachers in my rowdy state school who had themselves been educated at precisely the elite institution I would later join. But amongst my college friends, I know of no one who made that choice. For the most part, we were uninterested in what we considered to be 'unglamorous pursuits'. We valued individuality above all things. You can thank my generation for the invention of the word 'supermodel', and the popularisation of 'celebrity' and 'lifestyle', often used in conjunction with each other. Reality TV—that was us. Also televised talent shows. Also Ugg boots—you're welcome, millennials! And when the fussier amongst us detected in these visions of prestigious individuality perhaps something a little crass and commercialized, our solution was to go in some ways further down the same road, to out-individuate the celebrated individuals.

16 We became hipsters. Defined by the ways we weren't like everybody else. One amusing, much commented upon consequence of this was that we all ended up individuals of the same type. Not one-of-a-kind, but one . . . of a kind.

17 But there was another aspect I now find melancholic. We isolated ourselves. It took us the longest time to work out that we needed each other. You may have noticed that even now we seem somewhat stunned by quite ordinary human pursuits, like having children or living in a neighbourhood, or getting ill. We are always writing lifestyle articles about such matters in the Sunday papers. That's because, until very recently, we thought we were going to get through this whole life thing purely on our own steam. Even if we were no fans of the ex-British Prime Minister Margaret Thatcher, we had unwittingly taken her most famous slogan and embedded it deep within our own lives. "There is no such thing as society," she said. We were unique individuals. What did we need with society? But then it turned out that the things that have happened to everybody since the dawn of time also happened to us. Our parents got old and ill. Our children needed schools and somewhere to play. We wanted trains that ran on time. We needed each other. It turned out we were just human—like everybody.

18 Now I may have this completely backward, but I get the sense that something different is going on in your generation. Something hopeful. You seem to be smarter, sooner. Part of these smarts is surely born out of crisis. In the '90s we had high employment and a buoyant economy. We could afford to spend weeks wondering about the exact length and shape of our beards, or whether

Skill: Language, Style, and Audience

Smith mocks her generation, using simple words and nonstandard syntax. The sentences are brief, and the punctuation creates humorous pauses. This effectively conveys a lighthearted and informal tone.

Kurt Cobain[1] was a sell-out. Your situation is more **acute.** You have so many large, collective tasks ahead, and you know that. We had them too, but paid little attention, so now I'm afraid it falls to you. The climate, the economy, the sick relationship between the individual prestige of the first world and the anonymity of the third—these are things only many hands can fix working together. You are all individuals but you are also part of a generation and generations are defined by the projects they take on together.

Skill:
Textual Evidence

Smith focuses on the major issues faced by the current generation. She argues that these issues can only be solved by people working together. This textual evidence reveals how Smith sees the current generation as different from her own.

19 Even at the level of slogan you decided to honour the contribution of the many over the few, that now famous '99 Percent.'[2] As far as slogans go, which is not very far, yours still sounds more thoughtful to me than the slogans of my youth which were fatally infected by advertising. Be strong. Be fast. Be bold. Be different. Be you . . . be you, that was always the takeaway. And when my peers grew up, and went into advertising, they spread that message far and wide. "Just be you," screams the label on your shampoo bottle. "Just be you," cries your deodorant. "Because you're worth it." You get about fifty commencement speeches a day, and that's before you've even left the bathroom.

20 I didn't think you'd want any more of that from me. Instead I want to speak in favor of recognizing our place within 'the many'. Not only as a slogan, much less as a personal sacrifice, but rather as a potential source of joy in your life.

21 Here is a perhaps silly example. It happened to me recently at my mother's birthday. Around midnight it came time to divide up the rum cake, and I, not naturally one of life's volunteers, was press-ganged into helping. A small circle of women surrounded me, dressed in West African wraps and headscarves, in imitation of their ancestors. "Many hands make short work," said one, and passed me a stack of paper plates. It was my job to take the plated slices through the crowd. Hardly any words passed between us as we went about our collective task, but each time we set a new round upon a tray, I detected a hum of deep satisfaction at our many hands forming this useful human chain. Occasionally as I gave out a slice of cake, an older person would look up and murmur, "Oh you're Yvonne's daughter," but for the most part it was the cake itself that received the greeting or a little nod or a smile, for it was the duty of the daughter to hand out cake and no further commentary was required. And it was while doing what I hadn't realised was my duty that I felt what might be described as the exact opposite of the sensation I have standing in front of you now. Not puffed up with individual prestige, but immersed in the beauty of the crowd. Connected if only in gesture to an ancient line of practical women working in companionable silence in the

---

1. **Kurt Cobain** composer, singer, and guitarist Kurt Cobain (1967–1994) was front man of the Seattle post-punk band Nirvana
2. '**99 Percent** a populist term referring to the percentage of the American population that is not extremely wealthy

service of their community. It's such a ludicrously tiny example of the collective action and yet clearly still so rare in my own life that even this minor instance of it struck me.

Skill:
Language, Style,
and Audience

The repetition of the words *collective* and *individual* draws attention to the choice Smith thinks people must make. Throughout the speech, she posits that people can focus on individual goals or work as part of a group.

22   Anyway my point is that it was a beautiful feeling, and it was over too soon. And when I tried to look for a way to put it into this speech, I was surprised how difficult it is to find the right words to describe it. So many of our colloquial terms for this 'work of many hands' are sunk in infamy. 'Human chain' for starters; 'cog in the machine'; 'brick in the wall'. In such phrases we sense the long shadow of the twentieth century, with its brutal collective movements.

23   We do not trust the collective, we've seen what submission to it can do. We believe instead in the individual, here in America, especially. Now I also believe in the individual, I'm so grateful for the three years of college that helped make more or less of an individual out of me—teaching me how to think, and write. You may well ask, who am I to praise the work of many hands, when I myself chose the work of one pair of hands, the most isolated there is.

24   I can't escape that accusation. I can only look at my own habit of self love and ask, "what is the best use I can make of this utterly human habit?" Can I make a gift of myself in some other way? I know for sure I haven't done it half as much as I could or should have. I look at the fine example of my friend, the writer and activist Dave Eggers, and see a man who took his own individual prestige and parlayed it into an extraordinary collective action—826 National,[3] in which many hands work to create educational opportunities for disadvantaged kids all over this country.

25   And when you go to one of Dave's not-for-profit tutoring centres, you don't find selfless young people grimly sacrificing themselves for others. What you see is joy. Dave's achievement is neither quite charity nor simple individual philanthropy.[4] It's a collective effort that gets people involved in each other's lives.

26   I don't mean to speak meanly of philanthropy. Generally speaking, philanthropy is always better than no help at all, but it is also in itself a privilege of the few. And I think none of us want communities to rise or fall dependent upon the whims of the very rich. I think we would rather be involved in each other's lives and that what stops us, most often, is fear.

27   We fear that the work of many hands will obscure the beloved outline of our individual selves. But perhaps this self you've been treasuring for so long is

---

3. **826 National** a nationwide nonprofit organization founded by the writer Dave Eggers to encourage and help youth ages six to eighteen interested in writing
4. **philanthropy** voluntary promotion of human welfare, usually with money or influence

NOTES

itself the work of many hands. Speaking personally, I owe so much to the hard work of my parents, to the educational and health care systems in my country, to the love and care of my friends.

28   And even if one's individual prestige, such as it is, represents an entirely solo effort, the result of sheer hard work, does that everywhere and always mean that you deserve the largest possible slice of the pie?

29   These are big questions, and it is collectively that you'll have to decide them. Everything from the remuneration of executives to the idea of the commons itself depends upon it. And, at the core of the question, is what it really means to be 'the few' and 'the many'. Throughout your adult life you're going to have a daily choice to throw your lot in with one or the other. And a lot of people, most people, even people without the luxury of your choices, are going to suggest to you, over and over, that only an idiot chooses to join the many, when he could be one of the few.

30   Only an idiot chooses public over private, shared over gated, communal over unique. Mrs. Thatcher, who was such a genius at witty **aphorism,** once said, "A man who beyond the age of twenty-six, finds himself on a bus, can count himself a failure."

31   I've always been fascinated by that quote. By its dark assumption that even something as natural as sharing a journey with another person represents a form of personal denigration. The best reply to it that I know is that famous line of Terence, the Roman playwright. *Homo sum, humani nihil a me alienum puto.* 'I am a human being. I consider nothing that is human alien to me.'

32   Montaigne liked that so much he had it carved into the beams of his ceiling. Some people interpret it as a call to toleration. I find it stronger than that, I think it's a call to love. Now, full disclosure, most of the time I don't find it easy to love my fellow humans. I'm still that solipsistic 21-year-old. But the times I've been able to get over myself and get involved at whatever level, well what I'm trying to say is those have proved the most valuable moments of my life.

33   And I never would have guessed that back in 1997. Oh, I would have paid lip service to it, as a noble idea, but I wouldn't have believed it. And the thing is, it's not even a question of ethics or self-sacrifice or moral high ground, it's actually totally selfish. Being with people, doing for people, it's going to bring you joy. Unexpectedly, it just feels better.

34   It feels good to give your unique and prestigious selves a slip every now and then and confess your membership in this unwieldy collective called the human race.

35 For one thing, it's far less lonely, and for another, contra to Mrs. Thatcher, some of the best conversations you'll ever hear will be on public transport. If it weren't for the New York and London subway systems, my novels would be books of blank pages.

36 But I'm preaching to the converted. I see you, gazing into your phones as you walk down Broadway. And I know solipsism must be a constant danger, as it is for me, as it has been for every human since the dawn of time, but you've also got this tremendous, contrapuntal force propelling you into the world.

37 For aren't you always connecting to each other? Forever communicating, rarely scared of strangers, wildly open, ready to tell anyone everything? Doesn't online anonymity tear at the very idea of a prestige individual? Aren't young artists collapsing the border between themselves and their audience? Aren't young coders determined on an all-access world in which everybody is an equal participant? Are the young activists content just to raise the money and run? No. They want to be local, grassroots, involved. Those are all good instincts. I'm so excited to think of you pursuing them. Hold on to that desire for human connection. Don't let anyone scare you out of it.

38 Walk down these crowded streets with a smile on your face. Be thankful you get to walk so close to other humans. It's a privilege. Don't let your fellow humans be alien to you, and as you get older and perhaps a little less open than you are now, don't assume that exclusive always and everywhere means better. It may only mean lonelier. There will always be folks hard selling you the life of the few: the private schools, private planes, private islands, private life. They are trying to convince you that hell is other people. Don't believe it. We are far more frequently each other's shelter and correction, the antidote to solipsism, and so many windows on this world.

39 Thank you.

"New School Commencement Speech" by Zadie Smith. Published by The New School, 2014. Copyright © Zadie Smith. Reproduced by permission of the author c/o Rogers, Coleridge, & White Ltd., 20 Powis Mews, London W11 1JN

First Read

Read "Commencement Address at The New School." After you read, complete the Think Questions below.

 THINK QUESTIONS

1. How does Zadie Smith evaluate her own generation's experiences as compared to generations before and after? Explain, citing specific examples.

2. Why does Smith quote former British Prime Minister Margaret Thatcher at various points in her speech? What purpose does Thatcher serve in the address? Cite specific evidence from the text to support your answer.

3. What particular small event impressed on Smith the emotional value of shared work and contact with a community? Explain briefly, citing specific evidence from the text to support your response.

4. What is the meaning of the word **commodity** as it is used in the text? Write your best definition here. Then check an online or print dictionary, and compare your answer to the definition you find there.

5. Use context clues to determine the meaning of the word **aphorism** as it is used in the text. Write your definition here, and explain which clues helped you determine its meaning.

Please note that excerpts and passages in the StudySync® library and this workbook are intended as touchstones to generate interest in an author's work. The excerpts and passages do not substitute for the reading of entire texts, and StudySync® strongly recommends that students seek out and purchase the whole literary or informational work in order to experience it as the author intended. Links to online resellers are available in our digital library. In addition, complete works may be ordered through an authorized reseller by filling out and returning to StudySync® the order form enclosed in this workbook.

Reading & Writing Companion   117

Skill:
Language, Style, and Audience

Use the Checklist to analyze Language, Style, and Audience in "Commencement Address at The New School." Refer to the sample student annotations about Language, Style, and Audience in the text.

Copyright © Bookheaded Learning, LLC

••• CHECKLIST FOR LANGUAGE, STYLE, AND AUDIENCE

To determine an author's style and possible intended audience, do the following:

- ✓ Identify instances where the author uses key terms throughout the course of a text.

- ✓ Identify any particularly unusual, difficult, or effective syntax.

- ✓ Examine surrounding words and phrases to determine the context, connotation, style, and tone of the term's usage.

- ✓ Analyze how the author's treatment of the key term affects the reader's understanding of the text.

- ✓ Note the audience—both intended and unintended—and possible reactions to the author's word choice, style, and treatment of key terms.

To analyze how an author's treatment of language and key terms affects the reader's understanding of the text, consider the following questions:

- ✓ How do the author's word choices enhance or change what is being described?

- ✓ How do the author's word choices affect the reader's understanding of key terms and ideas in the text?

- ✓ How often does the author use this term or terms?

- ✓ How do choices about language affect the author's style and audience?

- ✓ How would the text be different with other words or different syntax? How does the author's use of varied syntax influence the meaning of the text?

Skill:
Language, Style, and Audience

Reread paragraphs 30–34 of "Commencement Address at The New School." Then use the Checklist on the previous page to answer the multiple-choice questions below.

⟳ YOUR TURN

1. In paragraph 31, Smith's choice to quote the Roman playwright Terence effectively—

   ○ A. shows off her knowledge of Latin in order to impress her audience with her intelligence.

   ○ B. encourages her listeners to focus on their own accomplishments and ignore others.

   ○ C. provides a counterpoint to Thatcher and emphasizes her own idea of what is truly important.

   ○ D. convinces her listeners that ancient Roman culture represented a high point in world history.

2. Which statement best evaluates how Smith uses language and style to affect the reader's/listener's perception of the relationship between individualism and collectivism?

   ○ A. Smith's repetition of the words *human* and *people* strongly reminds an audience of individuals that they are also part of a large group.

   ○ B. Smith's decision to include a funny quotation by Margaret Thatcher strongly suggests that people should avoid spending too much time with others.

   ○ C. Smith's concession that she does not always like other people strongly encourages the audience to focus on one another's individual faults.

   ○ D. Smith's wit and dismissive tone strongly suggest that the audience should not take her too seriously and should instead make up their own minds.

3. Which sentence from the excerpt contains a word order, or syntax, consisting of a subject followed by a verb followed by three objects?

   ○ A. "Only an idiot chooses public over private, shared over gated, communal over unique."

   ○ B. "Now, full disclosure, most of the time I don't find it easy to love my fellow humans."

   ○ C. "But the times I've been able to get over myself and get involved at whatever level, well what I'm trying to say is those have proved the most valuable moments of my life."

   ○ D. "Being with people, doing for people, it's going to bring you joy."

Skill:
Textual Evidence

Use the Checklist to analyze Textual Evidence in "Commencement Address at The New School." Refer to the sample student annotations about Textual Evidence in the text.

••• CHECKLIST FOR TEXTUAL EVIDENCE

To support an analysis by citing evidence that is explicitly stated in the text, do the following:

- ✓ Read the text closely and critically.

- ✓ Identify what the text says explicitly.

- ✓ Find the most relevant textual evidence that supports your analysis.

- ✓ Consider why an author explicitly states specific details and information.

- ✓ Cite the specific words, phrases, sentences, or paragraphs from the text that support your analysis.

- ✓ Determine where evidence in the text still leaves matters uncertain or unresolved.

To interpret implicit meanings in a text by making inferences, do the following:

- ✓ Combine information directly stated in the text with your own knowledge, experiences, and observations.

- ✓ Cite the specific words, phrases, sentences, or paragraphs from the text that led to and support this inference.

To cite textual evidence, as well as inferences drawn from the text, to support an analysis of what the text says explicitly, consider the following questions:

- ✓ Have I read the text closely and critically?

- ✓ What inferences am I making about the text?

- ✓ What textual evidence am I using to support these inferences?

- ✓ Am I quoting the evidence from the text correctly?

- ✓ Does my textual evidence logically relate to my analysis or the inference I am making?

- ✓ Does evidence in the text still leave certain matters unanswered or unresolved? In what ways?

Skill:
Textual Evidence

Reread paragraph 21 of "Commencement Address at The New School." Then use the Checklist on the previous page to answer the multiple-choice questions below.

 YOUR TURN

1. This question has two parts. First, answer Part A. Then, answer Part B.

   Part A: Which inference is best supported by this paragraph?

   ○ A. It is easy for a grown daughter to forget the duties she has toward her mother, particularly around a parent's birthday.

   ○ B. It is important for people to honor their ancestors by continuing to respect ancient customs, such as serving cake at a birthday party.

   ○ C. Working as part of a community creates something more beautiful and beneficial than working for individual recognition.

   ○ D. Even when the task is seemingly minor, performing a job in honor of one's parents represents an important step in becoming an adult.

   Part B: Which textual evidence from the paragraph best supports the answer to Part A?

   ○ A. "A small circle of women surrounded me, dressed in West African wraps and headscarves, in imitation of their ancestors."

   ○ B. "It was my job to take the plated slices through the crowd."

   ○ C. ". . . but for the most part it was the cake itself that received the greeting or a little nod or a smile, for it was the duty of the daughter to hand out cake and no further commentary was required."

   ○ D. "Connected if only in gesture to an ancient line of practical women working in companionable silence in the service of their community."

Please note that excerpts and passages in the StudySync® library and this workbook are intended as touchstones to generate interest in an author's work. The excerpts and passages do not substitute for the reading of entire texts, and StudySync® strongly recommends that students seek out and purchase the whole literary or informational work in order to experience it as the author intended. Links to online resellers are available in our digital library. In addition, complete works may be ordered through an authorized reseller by filling out and returning to StudySync® the order form enclosed in this workbook.

Reading & Writing
Companion

121

Skill:
Summarizing

Use the Checklist to analyze Summarizing in "Commencement Address at The New School." Refer to the sample student annotations about Summarizing in the text.

••• CHECKLIST FOR SUMMARIZING

To determine how to write an objective summary of a text, note the following:

✓ answers to the basic questions *who, what, where, when, why,* and *how*

✓ in literature or nonfiction, how the author develops two or more themes or central ideas over the course of the text and how they interact and build on one another to produce a complex account

✓ staying objective and not adding your personal thoughts, judgments, or opinions to the summary

To provide an objective summary of a text, consider the following questions:

✓ What are the answers to basic *who, what, where, when, why,* and *how* questions in literature and works of nonfiction?

✓ Does my summary include how the author develops two or more themes or central ideas over the course of the text and how these themes interact and build on one another?

✓ Is my summary objective, or have I added my thoughts, judgments, and personal opinions?

Skill:
Summarizing

Reread paragraphs 27–29 of "Commencement Address at The New School." Then use the Checklist on the previous page to answer the multiple-choice questions below.

⟳ YOUR TURN

1. How does this part of the speech build on main ideas throughout the speech?

   ○ A. Smith argues that we all depend on family, friends, and society and that group efforts make shared support and community possible.

   ○ B. Smith tells her audience they face the choice of being part of a community or part of the elite, just like Smith's generation did.

   ○ C. Smith points out that members of the developed world, like her audience, have many more choices and options than members of the developing world.

   ○ D. Smith argues that most people think it is a bad idea to seek to belong to a community when they could become a member of the ruling elite.

2. Which of the following is the most complete and unbiased summary of paragraphs 27–29?

   ○ A. Smith clearly conveys the idea that people cannot rise to the top without any help, and so she advocates for the value of community. However, she also recognizes that most people rightly view the choice to reject individuality as a silly one.

   ○ B. Smith argues that we often reject working with others because of the fear of being obscured. But most people are products of collective work, and it is an important choice to strive to be an individual or part of a community, even though many believe rejecting community is best.

   ○ C. Smith argues that successful people do not become successful completely on their own; they owe a lot to the support of their family, friends, and society.

   ○ D. Smith points out that even if people are able to achieve success completely on their own, they may not deserve more than everyone else. Smith tells her audience they will have to face the difficult choice of being poor and common or a member of the elite.

Please note that excerpts and passages in the StudySync® library and this workbook are intended as touchstones to generate interest in an author's work. The excerpts and passages do not substitute for the reading of entire texts, and StudySync® strongly recommends that students seek out and purchase the whole literary or informational work in order to experience it as the author intended. Links to online resellers are available in our digital library. In addition, complete works may be ordered through an authorized reseller by filling out and returning to StudySync® the order form enclosed in this workbook.

Reading & Writing Companion   123

Close Read

Reread "Commencement Address at The New School." As you reread, complete the Skills Focus questions below. Then use your answers and annotations from the questions to help you complete the Write activity.

1. Find a passage in which Smith uses a compare-and-contrast text structure to convey her ideas. Analyze whether the choice to use this structure helps the author make her ideas clear.

2. Highlight a passage in which Smith describes her attitude toward her generation. Summarize how details in the passage you selected develop two of the main ideas in the speech.

3. What can you infer is Zadie Smith's opinion of philanthropy? What are the positives and possible failures she sees in philanthropy? Find textual evidence to support your answer. Note where the textual evidence may leave matters unresolved.

4. Identify an example of vivid sensory language. Explain how Smith's choice to include these details effectively shapes the audience's perception of her main ideas.

5. Why is the generation graduating in 2014 so different from the class Zadie Smith graduated with in 1997? What are some of the causes that Zadie Smith identifies as the reasons things have changed so much between these generations? Cite textual evidence to support your answer.

PERSONAL RESPONSE: Most of Smith's commencement speech is about seeing oneself as one of the few or one of the many. React to this speech in a short essay. Use the examples Smith gives to summarize her central idea about individualism. Tell whether you plan to be one of the few or one of the many when you leave school. Explain your choice, using examples from your own life and textual evidence from Smith's speech.

Extended Oral Project and Grammar

EXTENDED ORAL PROJECT

Oral Presentation Process: Plan

PLAN	DRAFT	REVISE	EDIT AND PRESENT

The four years spent in high school undoubtedly changes graduates. The experiences they have, the knowledge they gain, and the memories they make will stay with them for a lifetime. Just as high school students change, the world around them changes, too. A common life goal is to leave the world a little better than you found it, whether that world is your high school, your community, or your country, for example.

WRITING PROMPT

What do future students need to know?

As your high school years now come to a close, think back on the last several years and consider the topics you have covered in all your subjects. Then consider the world around you now, and select a topic, an issue, a person, or an event that is important to you but that was not covered in your formal studies. Develop an argument to support the claim that this topic, issue, person, or event should be included in future high school instruction so the details and significance will be heard and remembered. To prepare for your presentation, consider how best to meet the needs of the audience, purpose, and occasion by employing the following:

- elements of classical speeches, including an introduction, a body, transitions, and a conclusion

- the art of persuasion and rhetorical devices

- the appropriate use of formal or informal language as well as purposeful vocabulary, tone, and voice

- visual aids that support the information presented, including citations and a works cited list for any information obtained from outside sources

- speaking techniques, such as eye contact, an appropriate speaking rate and volume, pauses for effect, enunciation, purposeful gestures, and appropriate conventions of language

Copyright © BookheadEd Learning, LLC

Introduction to Oral Presentation

Compelling oral presentations use both effective speaking techniques and engaging writing to express ideas and opinions. Oral presentations can have a variety of purposes, including persuasion. The characteristics of an effective argumentative oral presentation include:

- the organizational elements of classical speeches, including an introduction, a body, transitions, and a conclusion.

- the art of persuasion and rhetorical devices.

- the appropriate use of formal or informal language as well as purposeful vocabulary, tone, and voice.

- speaking techniques, such as eye contact, an appropriate speaking rate and volume, pauses for effect, enunciation, purposeful gestures, and appropriate conventions of language.

These characteristics can be organized into four major categories: context, structure, style and language, and elements of effective communication. As you continue with this Extended Oral Project, you'll receive more detailed instruction and practice in crafting each of the characteristics of argumentative writing and speaking to create your own oral presentation.

Please note that excerpts and passages in the StudySync® library and this workbook are intended as touchstones to generate interest in an author's work. The excerpts and passages do not substitute for the reading of entire texts, and StudySync® strongly recommends that students seek out and purchase the whole literary or informational work in order to experience it as the author intended. Links to online resellers are available in our digital library. In addition, complete works may be ordered through an authorized reseller by filling out and returning to StudySync® the order form enclosed in this workbook.

Reading & Writing Companion

127

Before you get started on your own oral presentation, read this oral presentation that one student, Josh, wrote in response to the prompt. As you read the Model, highlight and annotate the features of oral presentation writing that Josh included in his presentation.

NOTES

☰ STUDENT MODEL

Navigating the Digital World

By Josh

Introduction—Opening

My dad often jokes that my cell phone is glued to my hand. I do admit that I use my phone a lot, but almost everything I do is online. In the past 24 hours, I bought my grandmother a birthday present, took a history quiz, streamed three episodes of my favorite television show, ordered dinner, and researched the causes and effects of air pollution—all with a device in the palm of my hand.

Introduction—Claim

There are many advantages to living in the digital world, but we need to stop and consider how being online affects individuals and our society. Because a goal of any high school curriculum is to prepare students to enter the world, a contemporary high school education is not complete without lessons on living in a digital world.

Living in a Digital World

- We need to consider the online community's effects on individuals and society, both positive and negative.
- Schools should provide lessons on living in the digital world.

Body—Counterclaim

Some might believe that it is the responsibility of parents to teach their children how to be safe and smart online. I agree that parents should play a key role in teaching children how to navigate the internet, but not all parents are experts on the fast-paced digital world. That's why including formal instruction in media literacy in schools would ensure that all students learn how to be good online citizens.

For instance, if students studied the fact-checking guidelines that journalists use, they could enhance their media literacy. If everyone is going to participate in the digital world, then we should make sure that the digital world is a good place for everyone to be.

NOTES

Not Everyone Agrees

Some believe parents should be responsible.

- Not all parents are experts.
- Schools can provide formal instruction in media literacy.
- Students can learn how to fact-check what they discover online.

Body—Elaboration

At the click of a button, users can access the thoughts, opinions, and knowledge bases of millions of other people, whether they are located across town or across an ocean. People from all over the world weigh in on a myriad of topics on social media. This all might sound great; however, it is a double-edged sword.

Sometimes it is hard to know whether or not the information you read online is accurate, authoritative, and trustworthy. It should be our duty to make the internet better, safer, and more accurate for future generations.

At the same time, aspects of the internet, such as social media, can help create online communities that help people feel safe and heard, and also help them organize social action.

To accomplish this goal, schools need to teach students how to analyze and evaluate online sources and how to be responsible digital citizens. That means contributing to the digital space in a positive way, putting an end to cyberbullying, and stopping the propagation of false information.

The Online World Is a Double-Edged Sword

- How do I know whether or not the information I read online is accurate, authoritative, and trustworthy?
- Can social media help people feel safe and heard and also help them organize social action?
- How can schools help students become responsible digital citizens?

Body—Evidence and Analysis #1

While some people use the internet primarily to gain information, others go online to enact change.

Based on data collected by the Pew Research Center, Graph 1 demonstrates that there are various ways an individual can show that they are civically active on social media. The dark blue bar at the bottom of the graph indicates that 53% of U.S. adults have taken these actions, and the light blue bars show the percentage of people who have participated in specific activities on social media.

The most popular of these actions is taking part in a group of similarly minded activists on social media.

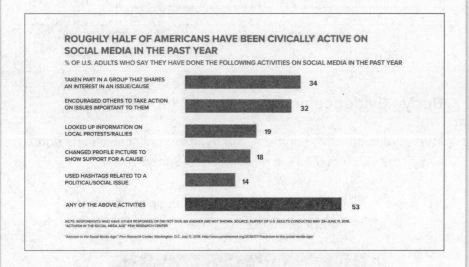

ROUGHLY HALF OF AMERICANS HAVE BEEN CIVICALLY ACTIVE ON SOCIAL MEDIA IN THE PAST YEAR

% OF U.S. ADULTS WHO SAY THEY HAVE DONE THE FOLLOWING ACTIVITIES ON SOCIAL MEDIA IN THE PAST YEAR

Activity	%
TAKEN PART IN A GROUP THAT SHARES AN INTEREST IN AN ISSUE/CAUSE	34
ENCOURAGED OTHERS TO TAKE ACTION ON ISSUES IMPORTANT TO THEM	32
LOOKED UP INFORMATION ON LOCAL PROTESTS/RALLIES	19
CHANGED PROFILE PICTURE TO SHOW SUPPORT FOR A CAUSE	18
USED HASHTAGS RELATED TO A POLITICAL/SOCIAL ISSUE	14
ANY OF THE ABOVE ACTIVITIES	53

NOTE: RESPONDENTS WHO GAVE OTHER RESPONSES OR DID NOT GIVE AN ANSWER ARE NOT SHOWN. SOURCE: SURVEY OF U.S. ADULTS CONDUCTED MAY 29–JUNE 11, 2018.
"ACTIVISM IN THE SOCIAL MEDIA AGE" PEW RESEARCH CENTER

"Activism in the Social Media Age" Pew Research Center, Washington, D.C. July 11, 2018. http://www.pewinternet.org/2018/07/11/activism-in-the-social-media-age/

Body—Evidence and Analysis #2

My next graph indicates that people believe these actions to be effective in specific ways.

Graph 2 also represents data collected by the Pew Research Center and shows that most Americans believe that social media is important to gain the attention of politicians. If we combine the "Very" (dark blue) and "Somewhat" (blue) bars, we see that around 60% of Americans say social media platforms are at least partly effective for getting politicians to pay attention to issues, creating activist movements, and influencing policy decisions.

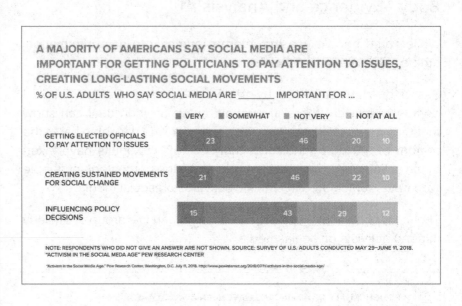

A MAJORITY OF AMERICANS SAY SOCIAL MEDIA ARE
IMPORTANT FOR GETTING POLITICIANS TO PAY ATTENTION TO ISSUES,
CREATING LONG-LASTING SOCIAL MOVEMENTS

% OF U.S. ADULTS WHO SAY SOCIAL MEDIA ARE _____ IMPORTANT FOR ...

	VERY	SOMEWHAT	NOT VERY	NOT AT ALL
GETTING ELECTED OFFICIALS TO PAY ATTENTION TO ISSUES	23	46	20	10
CREATING SUSTAINED MOVEMENTS FOR SOCIAL CHANGE	21	46	22	10
INFLUENCING POLICY DECISIONS	15	43	29	12

NOTE: RESPONDENTS WHO DID NOT GIVE AN ANSWER ARE NOT SHOWN. SOURCE: SURVEY OF U.S. ADULTS CONDUCTED MAY 29–JUNE 11, 2018.
"ACTIVISM IN THE SOCIAL MEDA AGE" PEW RESEARCH CENTER

"Activism in the Social Media Age." Pew Research Center, Washington, D.C. July 11, 2018. http://www.pewinternet.org/2018/07/11/activism-in-the-social-media-age/

Body—Evidence and Analysis #2 (continued)

These are impressive numbers, and even our political leaders agree (watch the video in the Plan lesson on the StudySync site):

President Obama Urges Public to Use
Social Media to Contact Senators

NBC News Archives Xpress

NOTES

Body—Evidence and Analysis #3

In addition, as Graph 3 demonstrates, social media is enabling citizens who had previously felt marginalized, including Hispanic and African American citizens, to find their voices and express their views.

As we can see by following the legend at the top of the graph, African American and Hispanic users are more likely than their white counterparts to state that social media platforms are effective for their activism.

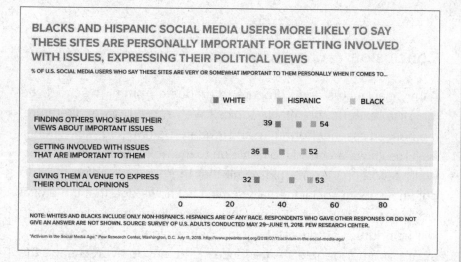

Body—Review

Although online activism can have positive effects by including a multitude of opinions, raising awareness, and promoting change, there can be many drawbacks, including people verbally attacking others and using dehumanizing speech.

Schools can help by teaching students how to evaluate the claims of online activists and how to participate effectively and respectfully in online activism.

Please note that excerpts and passages in the StudySync® library and this workbook are intended as touchstones to generate interest in an author's work. The excerpts and passages do not substitute for the reading of entire texts, and StudySync® strongly recommends that students seek out and purchase the whole literary or informational work in order to experience it as the author intended. Links to online resellers are available in our digital library. In addition, complete works may be ordered through an authorized reseller by filling out and returning to StudySync® the order form enclosed in this workbook.

Reading & Writing Companion

133

NOTES

A Brighter Future

- Bullying, hate speech, and misinformation are big challenges in the digital world.
- We can create a better internet by educating students to engage effectively.

Conclusion

As my classmates and I prepare to graduate from high school, we feel like experts on many topics. We've read great literature, memorized essential formulas, and repeated famous lab experiments. As a result, we are ready to move on to the next phases of our lives. While few teenagers would admit that there is something they do not know about social media, we must acknowledge that the digital world has many pitfalls. Formal lessons on living in the digital world will help future graduates become better digital citizens, be more aware of other people's experiences, and maybe even change the world.

Thank you!

Works Cited

"A majority of Americans say social media are important for getting politicians to pay attention to issues, creating long-lasting social movements." Pew Research Center, 10 July 2018, Washington, D.C., www.pewinternet. org/2018/07/11/public-attitudes-toward-political-engagement-on-social-media/pi_2018-07-10_social-activism_0-05/.

"Blacks and Hispanic social media users more likely to say these sites are personally important for getting involved with issues, expressing their political views." Pew Research Center, 10 July 2018, Washington, D.C., www.pewinternet.org/2018/07/11/public-attitudes-toward-political-engagement-on-social-media/pi_2018-07-10_social-activism_0-04/.

"President Obama Urges Public to Use Social Media to Contact Senators." NBC News Archives Xpress, NBC News, 29 July 2011,www.nbcnewsarchivesxpress.com/ contentdetails/214755.

"Roughly half of Americans have been civically active on social media in the past year." Pew Research Center, 10 July 2018, Washington, D.C., www.pewinternet.org/2018/07/11/public-attitudes-toward-political-engagement-on-social-media/pi_2018-07-10_social-activism_0-02/.

Please note that excerpts and passages in the StudySync® library and this workbook are intended as touchstones to generate interest in an author's work. The excerpts and passages do not substitute for the reading of entire texts, and StudySync® strongly recommends that students seek out and purchase the whole literary or informational work in order to experience it as the author intended. Links to online resellers are available in our digital library. In addition, complete works may be ordered through an authorized reseller by filling out and returning to StudySync® the order form enclosed in this workbook.

Reading & Writing Companion   135

✏ WRITE

When you write for an oral presentation, it is important to consider your audience and purpose so you can write appropriately for them. Your purpose is implied in the prompt. Reread the prompt to determine your purpose for writing and presenting.

To begin, review the questions below and then select a strategy, such as brainstorming, journaling, reading, or discussing, to generate ideas.

- **Purpose:** What topic, issue, person, or event will be the focus of your presentation, and what important ideas do you want to convey?

- **Audience:** Who is your audience, and what message do you want to express to your audience?

- **Thesis:** What claim will you communicate about the significance of this topic, issue, person, or event?

- **Evidence:** What facts, evidence, and details might you include to support your ideas? What research might you need to do? What anecdotes from your personal life or what background knowledge is relevant to the topic of your presentation?

- **Organization:** How can you organize your presentation so that it is clear and easy to follow?

- **Clear Communication:** How will you make sure that your audience can hear and understand what you are saying?

- **Gestures and Visual Aids:** What illustrations or other visual aids could you use during your presentation? What effect will they have on your audience? What physical gestures and body language will help you communicate your ideas?

Response Instructions

Use the questions in the bulleted list and the ideas you generated to write a one-paragraph summary. Your summary should describe what you will discuss in your oral presentation.

Don't worry about including all of the details now; focus only on the most essential and important elements. You will refer to this short summary as you continue through the steps of the writing process.

Skill: Organizing an Oral Presentation

To present information, findings, and supporting evidence that convey a clear and distinct perspective, do the following:

- Choose a style for your oral presentation, either formal or informal.

- Determine whether the development and organization of your presentation, as well as its substance and style, are appropriate for your purpose, audience, and task.

- Determine whether your presentation conveys a clear and distinct perspective so listeners can follow your line of reasoning.

- Make sure you address alternative perspectives that oppose your own in your presentation.

- Make strategic, or deliberate, use of digital media, such as textual, graphical, audio, visual, and interactive elements, to add interest and enhance your audience's understanding of the findings, reasoning, and evidence in your presentation.

To present information, findings, and supporting evidence that convey a clear and distinct perspective, consider the following questions:

- Did I make sure the information in my presentation conveys a clear and distinct perspective so listeners can follow my line of reasoning?

- Have I presented opposing or alternative viewpoints in my presentation?

- Are the organization, development, substance, and style appropriate for my purpose and audience?

- Have I made strategic use of media to add interest and enhance my audience's understanding of my presentation?

YOUR TURN

Read each sentence below. Then complete the chart on the next page by determining where each sentence belongs in the outline. Write the corresponding letter for each sentence in the appropriate row.

	Sentences
A	I will acknowledge the counterclaim that forming sleep habits is complicated by early start times at school, extracurricular activities in the evening, homework, and maintaining a social life. The school schedule can prevent teenagers from getting adequate sleep, regardless of screen time. However, screens can complicate sleep schedules even more, especially when it's so hard to find the time to rest.
B	I can include a graph that shows the relationship between sleep quality and energy levels.
C	I can use words like *next, thus,* and *additionally* to support the logical flow of ideas in my argument.
D	Everybody sleeps, but some people do it better than others. I can include an anecdote about struggling with getting enough sleep because I keep my phone next to me when I sleep. My thesis will state that students should learn sleep strategies to develop good habits and support their health.
E	I believe that this topic is important because lots of people are unaware of how screen usage affects sleep patterns. I also want to explain how good sleep habits lower your risk for serious health problems and increase your ability to think clearly and get along with others.
F	In the end, I will reiterate the importance of getting solid sleep each day. I will rephrase my thesis and summarize my main points.
G	I want to convince people that students should learn about forming good sleep habits.

Purpose	
Introduction/Thesis	
Alternative/Opposing Viewpoints	
Body	
Visual Aids	
Logical Progression	
Conclusion/Rephrasing of Thesis	

✏ WRITE

Use the questions in the Checklist to outline your oral presentation. Be sure to include a clear thesis and a logical progression of valid reasons.

Please note that excerpts and passages in the StudySync® library and this workbook are intended as touchstones to generate interest in an author's work. The excerpts and passages do not substitute for the reading of entire texts, and StudySync® strongly recommends that students seek out and purchase the whole literary or informational work in order to experience it as the author intended. Links to online resellers are available in our digital library. In addition, complete works may be ordered through an authorized reseller by filling out and returning to StudySync® the order form enclosed in this workbook.

Reading & Writing Companion **139**

Skill:
Evaluating Sources

••• CHECKLIST FOR EVALUATING SOURCES

As you reread the sources you gathered, identify the following:

- where information seems inaccurate, biased, or outdated
- where information strongly relates to your task, purpose, and audience
- where information helps you make an informed decision or solve a problem

To conduct advanced searches to gather relevant, credible, and accurate print and digital sources, use the following questions as a guide:

- Is the material published by a well-established source or expert author?
- Is the material up-to-date or based on the most current information?
- Is the material factual, and can it be verified by another source?
- Do discrepancies exist between the information presented in different sources?
- Can I use specific terms or phrases to adjust my search?

YOUR TURN

Choose the best answer to each question.

1. Josh finds an article titled "A Look at 2012: How Social Media Will Bring Us Together" that was published on a website his teacher recommended. What should Josh do to make sure he is reading a reliable source?

    ○ A. Josh should check all the information in the article to confirm it is still relevant today.

    ○ B. Josh should check whether the article contains too many counterclaims from experts on this topic.

    ○ C. Josh should decide whether he agrees with the arguments and reasons presented by the author.

    ○ D. Josh should check to make sure the article presents unique data and evidence.

2. Josh finds another article from 2018 titled "Social Media Will Ruin Us" published by *The Simpler Life*, a nationally distributed magazine. What should Josh consider before using this source?

    ○ A. The source may be outdated and contain information that is no longer relevant.

    ○ B. The source may be unreliable because it is printed in a nationally distributed magazine.

    ○ C. The source may be irrelevant to his thesis or presentation because it is about social media.

    ○ D. The source may be biased, given the title of the article and of the magazine in which it is published.

YOUR TURN

Complete the chart by filling in the title and author of a source for your presentation and answering the questions about it.

Source Title and Author:	
Reliability: Has the source material been published in a well-established book or periodical or on a well-established website? Is the source material up-to-date or based on the most current information?	
Accuracy: Is the source based on factual information that can be verified by another source? Do any discrepancies exist between this source and others?	
Credibility: Did a recognized expert on the topic write the source material? Did a well-respected author or organization publish the source material?	
Decision: Should I use this source in my presentation?	

Skill: Considering Audience and Purpose

••• CHECKLIST FOR CONSIDERING AUDIENCE AND PURPOSE

To present information so listeners can follow the line of reasoning and to ensure that the organization, development, substance, and style of your presentation are appropriate, do the following:

- When writing your presentation, convey and maintain a clear and distinct perspective or viewpoint.

- Make sure listeners can follow your line of reasoning, or the set of reasons you have used, so that your perspective is clear.

- Address any opposing or alternative perspectives.

- Check the development and organization of the information in your presentation to see that they are appropriate for your purpose, audience, and task.

- Determine whether the substance, or basis of your presentation, is also appropriate for your purpose, audience, and task.

- Remember to adapt your presentation to your task, and if it is appropriate, use formal English language you would use in ordinary conversation.

To better understand how to present information so listeners can follow the line of reasoning and to ensure that the organization, development, substance, and style of your presentation are appropriate, consider the following questions:

- Have I organized the information in my presentation so that my perspective is clear?

- Did I address any opposing or alternative perspectives?

- Have I developed and organized the information so it is appropriate for my purpose, audience, and task?

- Are the substance and style suitable?

YOUR TURN

Read each statement below. Then complete the chart by identifying whether the statements are appropriate for a formal presentation. Write the corresponding letter for each statement in the appropriate column.

	Statements
A	Horror movies can be real scary flicks.
B	Knowing basic first aid could help save lives.
C	Sewing not only encourages creativity, but it also improves manual dexterity.
D	My mom thinks video games are such a waste of time, but she's wrong.
E	The history of American television reflects the values, issues, and ideals of an ever-changing nation.
F	Frank Wills, this guy who helped uncover the Watergate scandal in 1972, is somebody people should know about.

Appropriate	Inappropriate

YOUR TURN

Complete the chart by answering each question about your presentation.

Question	My Response
What is my purpose, and who is my audience?	
Do I plan to use formal or informal language?	
How will I organize information so my perspective is clear?	
How will I address opposing or alternate perspectives?	
What sort of tone, or attitude, do I want to convey?	
How would I describe the voice I would like to use in my presentation?	
How will I use vocabulary and language to create that particular voice?	

Skill:
Persuasive Techniques

••• CHECKLIST FOR PERSUASIVE TECHNIQUES

In order to compose argumentative texts using genre characteristics and craft, use the following steps:

- First, consider your audience and purpose. You should ask yourself:

  > What does the audience already know or understand about my topic or argument? What possible biases does the audience hold?

  > What are the strengths and limitations of my argument?

  > What counterclaim(s) have I identified?

  > What are the strengths and limitations of each counterclaim?

- Next, consider the following persuasive techniques and the ways you might use one or more to reach your audience and achieve your purpose:

  > Appeals to Logic

     o   What findings or supporting evidence will I use to support my claim?

     o   What is the most effective way to present factual information to persuade my audience that my argument is logically sound and reasonable?

  > Appeals to Emotion

     o   What emotions do I want my audience to feel about my topic?

     o   What words or phrases should I include to bring about those feelings in my audience?

  > Appeals to Ethics

     o   Which experts could I use to establish the credibility of my claims?

     o   What words or phrases should I include to remind my audience of our shared values about what is right, good, and fair?

> Rhetorical Devices or Style

  o How can I use language in artful and persuasive ways to persuade my audience to accept my position?

  o What specific rhetorical devices, such as rhetorical questions, repetition, or parallelism, do I want to use to make my argument more persuasive?

> Counterclaim

  o What is an alternative or opposing perspective that my audience might have?

  o How can I rebut that opposing perspective in a way that respects my audience and strengthens my argument?

YOUR TURN

Read the appeals below. Then complete the chart by placing each appeal in the appropriate category. Write the corresponding letter for each appeal in the appropriate column.

	Appeals
A	If you care about your child's safety, you will buy this car seat.
B	Cell phone use leads to 1.6 million car crashes a year.
C	Drivers have a responsibility to keep everyone safe.
D	No one wants to suffer and have his or her life cut short from a disease caused by poor diet.
E	As a pediatrician, I provide my patients information on healthy eating.
F	Unhealthy eating and inactivity cause 678,000 deaths every year.

Appeal to Logic	Appeal to Emotion	Appeal to Ethics

WRITE

Use the questions in the Checklist to think about persuasive techniques you can use in your presentation. Then write a few sentences using persuasive techniques you might be able to include in your presentation.

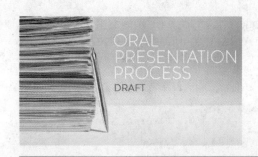

Oral Presentation Process: Draft

PLAN	DRAFT	REVISE	EDIT AND PRESENT

You have already made progress toward writing your argumentative oral presentation. Now it is time to draft your argumentative oral presentation.

 WRITE

Use your plan and other responses in your Binder to draft your argumentative oral presentation. You may also have new ideas as you begin drafting. Feel free to explore those new ideas as they occur to you. You can also ask yourself these questions to ensure that your writing is focused, organized, and developed with evidence and elaboration:

Draft Checklist:

- **Focus:** Is the topic of my presentation clear to my audience? Have I included only relevant information and details about my topic? Have I avoided extraneous details that might confuse or distract my audience?

- **Organization:** Is the organization of ideas and events in my presentation logical? Have I reinforced this logical structure with transitional words and phrases to help my audience follow the order of ideas? Do the sentences in my presentation flow together naturally? Will the sentences sound choppy or long-winded when I deliver them orally?

- **Evidence and Elaboration:** Do all my details support my thesis about why this topic, issue, person, or event should be included in high school instruction? Have I elaborated on the evidence to explain how it supports my thesis?

Before you submit your draft, read it over carefully. You want to be sure you've responded to all aspects of the prompt.

Here is Josh's argumentative oral presentation draft. As you read, notice how Josh develops his draft to be focused, organized, and developed with evidence and elaboration. As he continues to revise and edit his argumentative oral presentation, he will find and improve weak spots in his writing, as well as correct any language or punctuation mistakes.

NOTES

☰ STUDENT MODEL: FIRST DRAFT

Navigating the Digital World

My dad often jokes that my cell phone is glued to my hand. I do admit that I use my phone a lot, but almost everything I do is online. In the past 24 hours, all with a device in the palm of my hand, I bought my grandmother a birthday present, took a history quiz, streamed three episodes of my favorite television show, ordered dinner, and researched the causes and effects of air pollution. There are many advantages to living in the digital world, but we need to stop and consider how being online affects individuals and our society. Because a goal of any high school curriculum is to prepare students to enter the world, a contemporary high school education is not complete without lessons on living in a digital world.

~~Some might beleive that it is the responsibility of parents to teach their children how to be safe and smart online. I agree that parents should play a key role in teaching children how to navigate the internet. However, they cannot be the only solution. Let's be honest: parents are too out-of-touch to know everything there is to know about the fast-paced digital world. That's why including formal instruction in media literacy in schools would ensure that all students learn how to be good online citizens, for instance, if students studied the fact-checking guidelines that journalists use, they could enhance their media literacy and never fall trap to fake news again.~~

Body—Counterclaim
Some might believe that it is the responsibility of parents to teach their children how to be safe and smart online. I agree that parents should play a key role in teaching children how to navigate the internet, but not all parents are experts on the fast-paced digital world. That's why including formal instruction in media literacy in schools would ensure that all students learn how to be good online citizens.

For instance, if students studied the fact-checking guidelines that journalists use, they could enhance their media literacy. If everyone is going to participate in the digital world, then we should make sure that the digital world is a good place for everyone to be. [Show slide with bullet points.]

Skill:
Reasons and Evidence

The second paragraph of Josh's draft includes exaggeration and illogical reasoning, which undermine his argument. He revises his points to ensure that his reasoning is sound.

At the click of a button, users can access the thoughts, opinions, and knowledge bases of millions of other people, weather they are located across town or across an ocean. People from all over the world weigh in on a myriad of topics on social media. This all might sound great however, it is both a plus and a minus. Sometimes it is hard to know whether or not the information you read online is accurate, authoritative, and can be trusted. It should be our duty to make the internet better. More accurate for future generations. To accomplish this goal, schools need to teach students how to analyze and evaluate online sources and how to be responsible digital citizens.

As graphs 1 and 2 demonstrate, more and more Americans are using social media for the purpose of online activism and believe that social media is important to gain the attention of out-of-touch politicians. In addition, social media is enabling citizens who had previously felt marginalized to find their voices and express their views. Although online activism can have positive effects by including a multitude of opinions, raising awareness, and promoting change, there can be many bad effects, including people verbally attacking others and using dehumanizing speech. Schools can help avoid these disastrous and uncivil behaviors. [Show graphs that provide information about demographics and activities of social media users.]

Body—Evidence and Analysis #1
While some people use the internet primarily to gain information, others go online to enact change.

Based on data collected by the Pew Research Center, Graph 1 demonstrates that there are various ways an individual can show that they are civically active on social media. [Show Graph 1.] The dark blue bar at the bottom of the graph indicates that 53% of U.S. adults have taken these actions, and the light blue bars show the percentage of people who have participated in specific activities on social media.

The most popular of these actions is taking part in a group of similarly minded activists on social media.

Body—Evidence and Analysis #2
My next graph indicates that people believe these actions to be effective in specific ways. [Show Graph 2.]

Graph 2 also represents data collected by the Pew Research Center and shows that most Americans believe that social media is important to gain the attention of politicians. If we combine the "Very" (dark blue) and "Somewhat" (blue) bars, we see that around 60% of Americans say social media platforms are at least partly effective for getting politicians to pay attention to issues, creating activist movements, and influencing policy decisions.

Skill: Engaging in Discourse

Josh's partner tells him that the data in the graphs creates a strong logical appeal. Josh could strengthen the appeal, though, by providing a more detailed explanation of the graphs, which he decides to do.

Skill: Communicating Ideas

When Josh delivers his presentation, he'll point to the parts of the graphs that he's discussing. He'll use these gestures to focus the audience's attention on the information and help make the graphs clear.

Copyright © BookheadEd Learning, LLC

These are impressive numbers, and even our political leaders agree: [Show video of former President Obama.]

Body—Evidence and Analysis #3
In addition, as Graph 3 demonstrates, social media is enabling citizens who had previously felt marginalized, including Hispanic and African American citizens, to find their voices and express their views. [Show graph 3.]

As we can see by following the legend at the top of the graph, African American and Hispanic users are more likely than their white counterparts to state that social media platforms are effective for their activism.

As my classmates and I preparing to gradute from high school. we feel like experts on many topics I personally loved learning about the central nervous system thought learning about how the framers wrote the Constitution was really cool. We've read great literature, memorized formulas, and famous lab experiments. We are ready to move on to the next phases of our lives. Few teenagers would admit that there is something they do not know about social media. We must acknowledge that the digital world has many pitfalls. Formal lessons on living in the digital world will help future graduates a lot.

[Show a works cited slide.]

Sources

- Pew Center Research graphs that show demographics and activities of social media users:

  - http://www.pewinternet.org/2018/07/11/public-attitudes-toward-political-engagement-on-social-media/pi_2018-07-10_social-activism_0-02/

  - http://www.pewinternet.org/2018/07/11/public-attitudes-toward-political-engagement-on-social-media/pi_2018-07-10_social-activism_0-05/

  - http://www.pewinternet.org/2018/07/11/public-attitudes-toward-political-engagement-on-social-media/pi_2018-07-10_social-activism_0-04/

  - https://www.nbcnewsarchivesxpress.com/contentdetails/214755

- **Obama video:**

  - https://www.nbcnewsarchivesxpress.com/contentdetails/214755

Skill:
Sources and
Citations

Josh will include a citation on each slide containing information from an outside source. At the end of his presentation, he'll include a works cited slide, listing all the sources he used.

Skill:
Sources and Citations

In your oral presentation, provide citations for any information you obtained from an outside source. This includes the following:

- direct quotations

- paraphrased information

- tables and data

- images

- videos

- audio files

The citations in your presentation should be as brief and unobtrusive as possible. Follow these general guidelines:

- The citation should indicate the author's last name and the page number(s) on which the information appears (if the source has numbered pages), enclosed in parentheses.

- If the author is not known, the citation should list the title of the work and, if helpful, the publisher.

At the end of your presentation, include your works cited list, which should include all the texts you quote or reference directly in your presentation. Your works cited list should also follow the guidelines of a standard and accepted format, such as MLA. Below are the elements and the order in which they should be listed in works cited entries, according to the MLA style:

- author (followed by a period)

- title of source (followed by a period)

- container, or the title of the larger work in which the source is located (followed by a comma)

- other contributors (followed by a comma)

- version (followed by a comma)

- number (followed by a comma)

- publisher (followed by a comma)

- publication date (followed by a comma)
- location (followed by a comma)
- URL, without the "http://" (followed by a period)

Not all these elements will apply to each citation. Include only the elements that are relevant for the source.

To check that you have gathered and cited sources correctly, consider the following questions:

- Did I cite the information I found using a standard format to avoid plagiarism?
- Did I include all my sources in my works cited list?

↻ YOUR TURN

Read the elements and examples below. Then complete the chart by placing them in the correct order, according to the MLA style for a works cited list. Write the corresponding letter for each element and example in the appropriate column.

Elements and Examples	
A	publisher
B	"A Theatrical Moscow Trial Draws the Ire of Russia's Cultural Elite."
C	title of source
D	Atlantic Media Company,
E	URL
F	container
G	*The Atlantic,*
H	www.theatlantic.com/international/archive/2019/01/russian-artist-serebrennikov-culture-trial-moscow/580306/.
I	Nemtsova, Anna.
J	author
K	publication date
L	14 Jan. 2019,

Example	Element

Please note that excerpts and passages in the StudySync® library and this workbook are intended as touchstones to generate interest in an author's work. The excerpts and passages do not substitute for the reading of entire texts, and StudySync® strongly recommends that students seek out and purchase the whole literary or informational work in order to experience it as the author intended. Links to online resellers are available in our digital library. In addition, complete works may be ordered through an authorized reseller by filling out and returning to StudySync® the order form enclosed in this workbook.

Reading & Writing Companion 155

WRITE

Use the information in the Checklist to create or revise your citations and works cited list. Make sure to identify the source of each piece of researched information in your presentation. This will let your audience know that the information you are presenting is trustworthy. When you have completed your citations, compile a list of all your sources and write out your works cited list. Refer to the *MLA Handbook* as needed.

Skill:
Communicating Ideas

••• CHECKLIST FOR COMMUNICATING IDEAS

Follow these steps as you rehearse your presentation:

- **Eye Contact:** Practice looking up and making eye contact while you speak. Rehearse your presentation in front of a mirror, making eye contact with yourself. Consider choosing a few audience members to look at during your presentation, but scan the audience from time to time so it doesn't seem as if you're speaking directly to only two or three people.

- **Speaking Rate:** Record yourself so you can judge your speaking rate. If you find yourself speaking too fast, time your presentation and work on slowing down your speech. In addition, you might want to plan pauses in your presentation to achieve a specific effect.

- **Volume:** Be aware of your volume. Make sure that you are speaking at a volume that will be loud enough for everyone to hear you, but not so loud that it will be uncomfortable for your audience.

- **Enunciation:** Decide which words you want to emphasize, and then enunciate them with particular clarity. Emphasizing certain words or terms can help you communicate more effectively and drive home your message.

- **Purposeful Gestures:** Rehearse your presentation with your arms relaxed at your sides. If you want to include a specific gesture, decide where in your presentation it will be most effective, and practice making that gesture until it feels natural.

- **Conventions of Language:** Make sure that you are using appropriate conventions of language for your audience and purpose.

↻ YOUR TURN

Read the examples of students who are communicating their ideas below. Then complete the chart by first identifying the appropriate category for each example and then deciding whether the example illustrates effective or ineffective communication. Write the corresponding letter for each example in the appropriate place in the chart.

	Examples
A	A student stands up straight in clear view of his or her audience.
B	A student speaks very softly and rushes through the presentation, using a monotone voice.
C	A student does not look up from his or her notecards.
D	A student uses his or her hands to emphasize a particularly important point.
E	A student slouches and stands with his or her arms crossed.
F	A student begins her formal presentation by saying, "Hello. Today I will talk about rain forests."
G	A student allows his or her arms to hang limply and does not move at all.
H	A student makes eye contact with various members of the audience.
I	A student projects his or her voice, but does not shout. He or she pronounces words carefully and speaks at a slightly slower rate than used in normal conversation.
J	A student begins her formal presentation by saying, "Yo. I'mma talk about some trees."

Category	Example of Effective Communication	Example of Ineffective Communication
Posture		
Eye Contact		
Volume/Rate/Enunciation		
Gestures		
Language Conventions		

✏ WRITE

Practice delivering your presentation by yourself or in front of a partner.

As you present, do the following:

- Employ steady eye contact.
- Use an appropriate speaking rate and volume to clearly communicate your ideas.
- Use pauses and enunciation for clarity and effect.
- Use purposeful gestures to add interest and meaning as you speak.
- Maintain a comfortable, confident posture to engage your audience.
- Use language conventions appropriate for an argumentative presentation, and avoid slang or inappropriate speech.

If you are working with a partner, use the Checklist to evaluate your partner's communication of ideas.

When you finish giving your argumentative oral presentation, write a brief but honest reflection about your experience of communicating your ideas. Did you make good eye contact? Did you speak too quickly or too softly? Did you maintain a comfortable, confident posture? Did you use appropriate language? Did you struggle to incorporate gestures that looked and felt natural? How can you better communicate your ideas in the future?

Please note that excerpts and passages in the StudySync® library and this workbook are intended as touchstones to generate interest in an author's work. The excerpts and passages do not substitute for the reading of entire texts, and StudySync® strongly recommends that students seek out and purchase the whole literary or informational work in order to experience it as the author intended. Links to online resellers are available in our digital library. In addition, complete works may be ordered through an authorized reseller by filling out and returning to StudySync® the order form enclosed in this workbook.

Reading & Writing
Companion

159

Skill:
Reasons and Evidence

••• CHECKLIST FOR REASONS AND EVIDENCE

In order to identify a speaker's point of view, reasoning, and use of evidence and rhetoric, note the following:

- the stance, or position, the speaker takes on a topic
- whether the premise, or the basis of the speech or talk, is based on logical reasoning
- whether the ideas follow one another in a way that shows clear, sound thinking
- whether the speaker employs the use of exaggeration, especially when citing facts or statistics
- the speaker's choice of words, the points he or she chooses to emphasize, and the tone, or general attitude

In order to evaluate a speaker's point of view, reasoning, and use of evidence and rhetoric, consider the following questions:

- What stance, or position, does the speaker take? Is the premise based on sound, logical reasoning? Why or why not?
- Does the speaker use facts and statistics to make a point? Are they exaggerated?
- What points does the speaker choose to emphasize?
- How does the speaker's choice of words match the tone he or she wants to establish?

♻ YOUR TURN

Read each example of reasoning from a draft of Josh's oral presentation below. Then complete the chart by sorting the examples into two categories: those that are logical and those that are illogical. Write the corresponding letter for each example in the appropriate column.

	Examples
A	As students' access to all forms of media increases, so does their ability to navigate it responsibly.
B	A student's access to technology does not mean the student uses it appropriately or is a good digital citizen.
C	Becoming media literacy savvy is complicated because it requires time, resources, and training.
D	We can always tell teachers to become more media literacy savvy because they use technology each day in their classrooms.
E	Living in a digital world means being inundated with both fake and legitimate news on a daily basis, but discerning fact from fiction can be tricky.
F	If a person doesn't know how to distinguish fake news from legitimate information, he or she is not trying.

Logical Reasoning	Illogical Reasoning

Please note that excerpts and passages in the StudySync® library and this workbook are intended as touchstones to generate interest in an author's work. The excerpts and passages do not substitute for the reading of entire texts, and StudySync® strongly recommends that students seek out and purchase the whole literary or informational work in order to experience it as the author intended. Links to online resellers are available in our digital library. In addition, complete works may be ordered through an authorized reseller by filling out and returning to StudySync® the order form enclosed in this workbook.

Reading & Writing Companion 161

YOUR TURN

Below are three examples of an ineffective use of evidence from a previous draft of Josh's oral presentation. In the second column, rewrite the sentences to use the evidence effectively, without exaggeration or faulty reasoning. The first row has been completed for you as an example.

Ineffective Use of Evidence	Effective Use of Evidence
Technology has made things like home security systems possible. We know that thanks to technology, the world is a safer place.	There are many advantages to living in the digital world, including technological advances that make us safer, such as home security systems.
According to Nonprofit Tech for Good, 51 percent of wealthy donors prefer to give online. This shows that social media is so powerful that it could ensure Americans vote in every election.	
Studies show that most people are skeptical of the information they read on the internet. According to my father, past generations believed everything they read, heard, or saw.	

Skill:
Engaging in Discourse

••• CHECKLIST FOR ENGAGING IN DISCOURSE

You and a partner will take turns practicing your argumentative oral presentations and giving feedback. The feedback you provide should be meaningful and respectful. That is, you should offer an honest assessment as well as specific tips for improvement, while using kind and considerate language.

In your feedback, make sure to evaluate and critique the speaker using these categories. Remember to always start by telling the speaker what he or she did particularly well.

Positive Points:

*   What is most effective about the oral presentation?
*   What strong points does the speaker make?
*   Which particular phrases are well written and memorable?

Clarity:

*   Does the speaker express his or her ideas in a clear, understandable way?
*   What changes can the speaker make to improve the clarity of his or her message?

Evidence and Elaboration:

*   Does the speaker offer a range of positions on his or her topic or issue?
*   Is there an opportunity to clarify, verify, or challenge ideas and conclusions made in the argument?
*   Does the speaker resolve contradictions in his or her argument?
*   Does the speaker use transitions and explanations effectively to show the relationship between ideas?
*   Where can the speaker add transitions or explanations to improve the logical flow of his or her message?
*   What additional information or research is required to deepen his or her message?

Diction:

*   Does the speaker's choice of words have an impact, or a strong effect?
*   Where can the speaker improve his or her word choice to create a stronger impact?

Syntax:

- Does the speaker use sentence construction to create a strong impact?

- Where can the speaker use sentence-construction techniques, such as ending a sentence with the most important idea, to improve the impact of his or her syntax?

Rhetorical Strategies:

- Does the speaker use language persuasively?

- Where can the speaker employ specific techniques, such as appeals to logic, emotion, and ethics, to improve the impact of his or her presentation?

YOUR TURN

Read each example of feedback below. Then complete the chart by placing the examples in the appropriate category. Write the corresponding letter for each example of feedback in the appropriate row. Some examples may belong in more than one category.

Feedback	
A	I'm not sure what you mean by "these strategies." Can you elaborate?
B	I think this sentence would be stronger if you moved the most important phrase to the end.
C	The wording of this sentence is a little vague. You might consider using more topic-specific vocabulary.
D	You make a good point here, but it would be stronger if you added a quote from a credible source.
E	I liked how you used an anecdote to make your opening more memorable.
F	The word *however* shows a strong connection between your ideas and evidence in this paragraph.

Category	Feedback
Positive Points	
Clarity	
Evidence and Elaboration	
Diction	
Syntax	
Rhetorical Strategy	

✏️ WRITE

Take turns reading your presentation aloud to a partner. When you finish, write a reflection about your experience of giving feedback. How did you ensure that your feedback was both meaningful and respectful? What did you do well? How can you improve in the future?

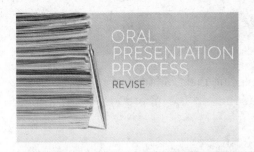

Oral Presentation Process: Revise

| PLAN | DRAFT | REVISE | EDIT AND PRESENT |

You have written a draft of your argumentative oral presentation. You have also received input from your peers about how to improve it. Now you are going to revise your draft and prepare your presentation by creating or revising slides and visuals to support your argument.

⬅ REVISION GUIDE

Examine your draft to find areas for revision. Keep in mind your purpose and audience as you revise for clarity, development, organization, and style. Also examine your draft to find slides that might need additional clarification or revision. For example, when Josh revised his presentation, he paid careful attention to how the content of each slide supported his thesis and message. Use the guide below to help you review.

Review	Revise	Example
Clarity		
Highlight each sentence that connects to your thesis statement.	Make sure the claim is clear for your audience in both your introduction and conclusion. Add headings to your presentation slides to clarify your ideas and claims for your audience, and simplify your ideas by turning them into brief bullet points.	Formal lessons on living in the digital world will help future graduates ~~a lot~~ become better digital citizens, be more aware of other people's experiences, and maybe even change the world.

Review	Revise	Example
Development		
Identify and annotate places in your presentation where your thesis is not supported by details.	Add details that strongly support the reasons for your claim. Include images, graphs, videos, and other visual elements that support your argument in your presentation. Think about places where a visual aid might replace text.	To accomplish this goal, schools need to teach students how to analyze and evaluate online sources and how to be responsible digital citizens. That means contributing to the digital space in a positive way, putting an end to cyberbullying, and stopping the propagation of false information.
Organization		
Syntax can help you emphasize ideas. Identify strong words and phrases that show your main ideas, and place them strategically.	Revise sentences so that the most important word or phrase comes at the end. Think about places where a visual aid might enhance a section of the presentation.	In the past 24 hours, ~~all with a device in the palm of my hand,~~ I bought my grandmother a birthday present, took a history quiz, streamed three episodes of my favorite television show, ordered dinner, and researched the causes and effects of air pollution.~~:~~—all with a device in the palm of my hand.
Style: Word Choice		
Identify key words and phrases that connect ideas across sentences. Annotate places where more precise language would strengthen the connection.	Replace vague or awkward words and phrases with precise ones that emphasize the connections between your ideas.	Online activism can have positive effects by including a multitude of opinions, raising awareness, and promoting change. However, there can be many drawbacks ~~bad effects~~, including people verbally attacking others and using dehumanizing speech.

Review	Revise	Example
Style: Sentence Fluency		
Read your presentation aloud, and listen to the way the text sounds. Does it sound choppy? Or does it flow smoothly with rhythm, movement, and emphasis on important details and events?	Shorten a group of long sentences, or join shorter sentences together using conjunctions and/or dependent clauses.	~~We~~ As a result, we are ready to move on to the next phases of our lives. ~~Few~~ While few teenagers would admit that there is something they do not know about social ~~media. We~~ media, we must acknowledge that the digital world has many pitfalls.

✎ WRITE

Use the Revision Guide, as well as your peer reviews, to help you evaluate your argumentative oral presentation to determine places you should revise.

Grammar: Parallel Structure

Parallel Structure

Parallel structure, or parallelism, is the deliberate repetition of words, phrases, or sentence structures of equal weight or importance.

Not Parallel	Parallel
The soup was hot, wholesome, and **tasted delicious**.	The soup was hot, wholesome, and **delicious**.
After dinner, Kevin completed his Spanish homework, wrote his English essay, and **has studied** for his math test.	After dinner, Kevin completed his Spanish homework, wrote his English essay, and **studied** for his math test.
Peter opened the world almanac, **checking the index**, and identified the capital of Rwanda.	Peter opened the world almanac, **checked the index**, and identified the capital of Rwanda.

Parallelism is a rhetorical device that helps emphasize ideas, establish rhythm, and make a text or speech more memorable. The examples below are from "Be Ye Men of Valour," a speech British Prime Minister Winston Churchill delivered in 1940 at a critical time during World War II.

Text	Explanation
I speak to you for the first time as Prime Minister in a solemn hour for the life of **our country, of our empire, of our allies, and**, above all, **of the cause of freedom**. . . . I am sure I speak for all when I say we are ready **to face it, to endure it, and to retaliate against it** to any extent that the unwritten laws of war permit. . . . We must have, and have quickly, **more aeroplanes, more tanks, more shells, more guns**. Be Ye Men of Valour	Churchill uses parallelism in lists for its rhetorical effect. • Parallel prepositional phrases emphasize the gravity of the *solemn hour* Churchill cites. • The parallel series of infinitive phrases emphasizes the readiness of Churchill and the people to whom he speaks. • The deliberate repetition of *more* in the list of elements needed emphasizes the immediacy of the country's need for equipment and ammunition.

↻ YOUR TURN

Choose the best answer to each question.

1. How should this sentence be changed to achieve parallel structure?

> He regretted staying up past midnight, eating an entire pizza by himself, and placing phone calls to old friends early in the morning.

○ A. Replace *he regretted* with *regretting*.
○ B. Replace *staying* with *stayed*.
○ C. Replace *placing* with *placed*.
○ D. No change needs to be made to this sentence.

2. How should this sentence be changed to achieve parallel structure?

> Sarah set the table, lit the candles, and waiting for her date to arrive.

○ A. Insert *and* after *table*.
○ B. Delete *lit the candles*.
○ C. Replace *waiting* with *waited*.
○ D. No change needs to be made to this sentence.

3. How should this sentence be changed to achieve parallel structure?

> David couldn't fall asleep because the TV was blaring, the shouting children, and the dog was barking.

○ A. Replace *TV was blaring* with *blaring TV*.
○ B. Replace *shouting children* with *children were shouting*.
○ C. Replace *dog was barking* with *barking dog*.
○ D. No change needs to be made to this sentence.

4. How should this sentence be changed to achieve parallel structure?

> She watched how the wind shifted, parting clouds, and streaming sunlight.

○ A. Change *how the wind shifted* to *how the shifting wind*.
○ B. Change *how the wind shifted* to *the shifting wind*.
○ C. Replace *and* with *with*.
○ D. No change needs to be made to this sentence.

Grammar:
Sentence Variety - Openings

Sentence Openers

Successful writers understand that ideas are not the only important aspect of writing; what's equally important is how those ideas are communicated. Varying your syntax is one way to help a reader remain engaged in what you are trying to say. One way to do this is to use a variety of sentence openers throughout your writing. Sentence openers help a reader more clearly understand the connection between sentences. The following strategies can help you vary the types of sentence openers you use:

Strategies	Text
Use a prepositional phrase to begin a sentence.	On the enclosed porch at the back of the house, a crisp white bag still sat on the wicker chaise, filled with lace she had once planned to turn into curtains. A Temporary Matter
Use an adverb to begin a sentence.	Generally speaking, philanthropy is always better than no help at all, but it is also in itself a privilege of the few. Commencement Address at The New School
Use a verb ending in *-ed* or *-ing* to begin a sentence.	Finding news and information has never been easier, and access is expanding to more people every day. News Literacy in the Misinformation Age
Use a very short sentence, which can help emphasize an important point or create excitement.	He looked relieved. Ghosts
Use words that correspond to time or a sequence of events to begin a sentence.	At the stroke of the midnight hour, when the world sleeps, India will awake to life and freedom. Tryst with Destiny

⟳ YOUR TURN

Choose the best answer to each question.

1. How should this sentence be edited to use transitional words as a sentence opener?

   > The new CEO took over and began to make many necessary changes.

   - ○ A. Frighteningly, the new CEO took over and began to make many necessary changes.
   - ○ B. As a result, the new CEO took over and began to make many necessary changes.
   - ○ C. Behind closed doors, the new CEO took over and began to make many necessary changes.
   - ○ D. No change needs to be made to this sentence.

2. How should this sentence be edited to use an adverb as a sentence opener?

   > Luckily, I made it to the meeting on time.

   - ○ A. I made it to the meeting on time, luckily.
   - ○ B. I am lucky that I made it to the meeting on time.
   - ○ C. I luckily made it to the meeting on time.
   - ○ D. No change needs to be made to this sentence.

3. How should this sentence be edited to make the sentence opener clearer?

   > People live in cities.

   - ○ A. Cities are places where people live.
   - ○ B. The people live in cities.
   - ○ C. Many people live in cities.
   - ○ D. No change needs to be made to this sentence.

4. How should this sentence be edited to use a sentence opener that corresponds to time?

   > The first scholar to edit Emily Dickinson's poems collected all of them into a single edition.

   - ○ A. The poems of Emily Dickinson were all collected into a single edition by a scholar.
   - ○ B. Surprisingly, the first scholar to edit Emily Dickinson's poems collected all of them into a single edition.
   - ○ C. Several decades later, the first scholar to edit Emily Dickinson's poems collected all of them into a single edition.
   - ○ D. No change needs to be made to this sentence.

Oral Presentation Process: Edit and Present

PLAN	DRAFT	REVISE	EDIT AND PRESENT

You have revised your oral presentation based on your peer feedback and your own examination.

Now it is time to edit your argumentative oral presentation. When you revised, you focused on the content of your oral presentation. You practiced strategies for citing your sources, communicating your ideas, presenting strong reasons and evidence, and engaging in discourse. When you edit, you focus on the mechanics of your oral presentation, paying close attention to language, syntax, and rhetorical devices that can be heard by your audience while you are talking.

Use the checklist below to guide you as you edit:

☐ Have I included a variety of sentence openers in my presentation?

☐ Have I used parallel structure to emphasize ideas, establish rhythm, and make my text or presentation more memorable?

☐ Have I used language that is too informal for my presentation?

☐ Have I added digital media strategically to enhance my presentation?

☐ Do I have any sentence fragments or run-on sentences?

☐ Have I spelled everything correctly?

Notice some edits Josh has made:

- Edited a sentence to correct a sentence fragment and use transitional words as a sentence opener

- Fixed a misspelled word

- Deleted a run-on sentence

- Changed a sentence to achieve parallel structure

As my classmates and I ~~preparing~~ prepare to ~~gradute~~ graduate from high school~~,~~ we feel like experts on many topics. ~~I personally loved learning about the central nervous system I thought learning about how the framers wrote the Constitution was really cool.~~ We've read great literature, memorized essential formulas, and repeated famous lab experiments. As a result, we are ready to move on to the next phases of our lives.

✏ WRITE

Use the Checklist, as well as your peer reviews, to help you evaluate your oral presentation to determine places that need editing. Then edit your presentation to correct those errors. Finally, rehearse your presentation, including both the delivery of your written work and the strategic use of the digital media you plan to incorporate.

After you have made all your corrections and rehearsed with your digital media selections, you are ready to present your work. You may present to your class or to a group of your peers. You can record your presentation to share with family and friends or post it on your blog. If you publish online, share the link with your family, friends, and classmates.

PHOTO/IMAGE CREDITS:

cover, iStock.com/
p. iii, iStock.com/DNY59
p. ix, iStock.com/
p. x, Leila Aboulela - Massimiliano Donati/
Awakening/Contributor/Getty Images Entertainment
p. x, Chimamanda Ngozi Adichie - Taylor Hill/
Contributor/FilmMagic/Getty Images
p. x, Jamaica Kincaid - Paul Marotta/Contributor/
Getty Images Entertainment
p. x, Jhumpa Lahiri - Venturelli/Contributor/GC
Images/Getty
p. x, Jawahalral Nehru - Margaret Bourke-White/
Contributor/The LIFE Picture Collection/Getty
Images
p. xi, Nelson Mandela - Ulrich Baumgarten/
Contributor/Ulrich Baumgarten/Getty
p. xi, Zadie Smith - Brian Dowling/Stringer/Getty
Images Entertainment
p. xi, Derek Walcott - Ulf Andersen/Contributor/
Hulton Archive/Getty
p. xii, iStock.com/pawopa3336
p. 1, Hulton Deutsch/Corbis Historical/Getty Images
p. 3, Tristan Fewings/Getty Images Entertainment/
Getty Images
p. 5, iStock.com/pawopa3336
p. 6, iStock.com/yangphoto
p. 7, Roberto Ricciuti/Getty Images Entertainment/
Getty Images
p. 9, iStock.com/yangphoto
p. 10, iStock.com/ValentinaPhotos
p. 11, iStock.com/ValentinaPhotos
p. 12, iStock.com/yangphoto
p. 13, iStock.com/TonyBaggett
p. 16, iStock.com/TriniJacobs
p. 18, Hindustan Times/Hindustan Times/Getty
Images
p. 21, iStock.com/TriniJacobs
p. 22, iStock.com/pixhook
p. 23, iStock.com/pixhook
p. 24, iStock.com/TriniJacobs
p. 25, istock.com/Devasahayam Chandra Dhas
p. 28, /AFP/Getty Images
p. 30, ©istock.com/shayes17
p. 33, iStock.com/urfinguss
p. 35, New York Times Co./Archive Photos/Getty
Images
p. 36, Jared Siskin/Patrick McMullan/Getty Images
p. 37, iStock/Konstik
p. 39, iStock.com/urfinguss
p. 40, iStock.com/peeterv
p. 41, STEPHANE DE SAKUTIN/AFP/Getty Images

p. 52, iStock.com/peeterv
p. 53, iStock.com/urbancow
p. 54, iStock.com/urbancow
p. 55, iStock.com/LdF
p. 56, iStock.com/LdF
p. 57, iStock.com/peeterv
p. 58, ©iStock.com/borchee
p. 59, Ulf Andersen/Hulton Archive/Getty Images
p. 61, iStock.com/GypsyGraphy
p. 62, Massimiliano Donati/Awakening/Getty Images
Entertainment/Getty Images"
p. 77, iStock.com/heibaihui
p. 78, Venturelli/GC Images/Getty Images"
p. 94, iStock.com/heibaihui
p. 95, iStock.com/Dominique_Lavoie
p. 96, iStock.com/Dominique_Lavoie
p. 97, iStock.com/LdF
p. 98, iStock.com/LdF
p. 99, iStock.com/heibaihui
p. 100, Education Images/Contributor/Universal
Images Group/GettyImages"
p. 109, istock.com/steinphoto
p. 117, istock.com/steinphoto
p. 118, iStock.com/antoni_halim
p. 119, iStock.com/antoni_halim
p. 120, iStock.com/urbancow
p. 121, iStock.com/urbancow
p. 122, iStock.com/
p. 123, iStock.com/
p. 124, istock.com/steinphoto
p. 125, iStock.com/hanibaram, iStock.com/seb_ra,
iStock.com/Martin Barraud
p. 126, iStock.com/Martin Barraud
p. 131, StudySync Graphic
p. 132, NBC Universal Archives
p. 133, StudySync Graphic
p. 137, iStock.com/BilevichOlga
p. 140, iStock.com/Mutlu Kurtbas
p. 143, iStock.com/
p. 146, iStock.com/DNY59
p. 149, iStock.com/Martin Barraud
p. 153, iStock.com/tofumax
p. 157, iStock.com/polesnoy
p. 163, iStock.com/SasinParaksa
p. 166, iStock.com/Martin Barraud
p. 169, iStock.com/Vimvertigo
p. 171, iStock.com/mooltfilm
p. 173, iStock.com/Martin Barraud

studysync

Text Fulfillment Through StudySync

If you are interested in specific titles, please fill out the form below and we will check availability through our partners.

ORDER DETAILS

Date:

TITLE	AUTHOR	Paperback/ Hardcover	Specific Edition *If Applicable*	Quantity

SHIPPING INFORMATION

Contact:

Title:

School/District:

Address Line 1:

Address Line 2:

Zip or Postal Code:

Phone:

Mobile:

Email:

BILLING INFORMATION   ☐ *SAME AS SHIPPING*

Contact:

Title:

School/District:

Address Line 1:

Address Line 2:

Zip or Postal Code:

Phone:

Mobile:

Email:

PAYMENT INFORMATION

☐ CREDIT CARD

Name on Card:

Card Number: Expiration Date: Security Code:

☐ PO

Purchase Order Number:

StudySync Text Fulfillment, BookheadEd Learning, LLC
610 Daniel Young Drive | Sonoma, CA 95476